A JOURNEY OF THE HEART:
The Call to Teaching

by
E. Grady Bogue

Professor and Chancellor Emeritus
Louisiana State University at Shreveport

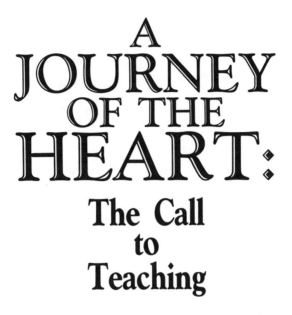

25th Anniversary
EDUCATIONAL
FOUNDATION
An Investment in
Tomorrow

A Silver Anniversary Publication of the
Phi Delta Kappa Educational Foundation
Bloomington, Indiana

Cover design by Victoria Voelker

Library of Congress Catalog Card Number 91-60523
ISBN 0-87367-448-0
0-87367-449-9 (pbk.)

Dedication

To those men and women in this nation who are
called to a journey of the heart — to teachers in your
life and mine.

This monograph is sponsored by the Phi Delta Kappa District VI Representative and area coordinators, who made a generous contribution toward publication costs.

They sponsor this monograph to honor the memory of Area 6G Coordinator Wayne R. King, friend and colleague, loyal Kappan, and caring and sensitive educator. A specialist in counseling and the social sciences and a connoisseur of the theater and art, Wayne R. King was deeply committed to serving youth, to educational excellence, and to the Phi Delta Kappa ideals of leadership, research, and service. His counsel and his warmth and understanding will be missed by all who were fortunate to know him.

James V. Fogarty, Jr., District VI Representative

District VI Coordinators:

Michael J. Dorgan
Richard R. Grandey
Dominic Natoli, Jr.
Carolyn J. Nieset
Joel R. Oppenheim
Steven A. Pavlak
Luther W. Pfluger
Ranny Singiser

John M. Skalski
Karol Strelecki
Ronald S. Sullivan
John K. Taylor
Evelyn Valentine
William J. Vaugh
Robert C. White

Acknowledgments

I am indebted to several friends and colleagues who made this book possible:

To Cody White and the Powers Foundation, who invested in this work.

To Sue Carroll, Jackie Reed, and Susan Jusselin, who gave birth to the manuscript and endured with patience and cheer the endless changes and corrections.

To the many school professionals and colleagues cited in this work, who gave of their time and their life models.

To my wife and children, who experienced the early morning interruptions in our family life as I pecked away on my computer and wandered the house in the wee hours of the morning.

To editor and friend Derek L. Burleson, who with sharp wit and pen helped to make a strengthened work in this our second venture.

Thanks to each and every one for your support.

Table of Contents

Preface

In legislative chambers, in major books and reports, in media coverage, in conferences at every level of our national life, there is a lively renaissance of interest in American education. Pupil test scores and school effectiveness, teacher salaries and teacher credentials, tuition tax credits and vouchers, national education goals and accountability — the public policy issues are before us in frequent forums.

Much of the coverage is critical. I make no case that criticism is not needed. It is. In fact, our schools have been singularly successful in at least one worthwhile goal — producing graduates who are astute critics of all aspects of our national life.

What does all this national policy ferment look like to the special education teacher changing the diaper of a retarded 14-year-old, to the beginning elementary teacher entering a 99-degree classroom in a difficult neighborhood, to the 20-year veteran teaching mathematics in a rural high school, to the soon-to-retire college history professor?

The standards of our schools and the performance of our students rest in the hearts and minds of those who teach. Yet we have few contemporary sources that celebrate the special call to teaching, that provide an intimate and inspiring glimpse into the pleasure and the pain of teaching. Among those works that do, and which are close to my heart, are Delderfield's fictional work, *To Serve Them All My Days* (1972), Conroy's *The Water Is Wide* (1972), Highet's *The Immortal Profession* (1976), Goodlad's *A Place Called School* (1984), and Stuart's *To Teach, To Love* (1970). But among the plethora of other contemporary reports, there are few that look at the world of teaching and learning from inside the classroom, few examples that represent the personal and poignant moments of those who labor there. Two recent notable exceptions are Tracy Kidder's *Among School-children* (1989) and Samuel Freedman's *Small Victories* (1990).

The essays in this volume are intended to give visibility to the nature and nobility of teaching — a reflective celebration of the call to teaching. My mother was a 19-year-old teacher in a one-room rural West

Tennessee school more than half a century ago. My sister is a 20-year veteran of elementary teaching in a small West Tennessee town not 10 miles from where my mother taught. She does more good in a day than I will in a year. She will show up on the porch of any parent, rich or poor, who is neglecting a child. And she has been known to liven up the day of both principals and superintendents who were not caring for the schools in which she served.

I am concluding a quarter-century as teacher and administrator. I am an educator by choice. For me, just one mind, heart, or spirit damaged by ignorance is one too many. Teaching is a precious work. It is one human endeavor completely positive and constructive in outcome when rightly done. It also is the one human endeavor most damaging in consequence when done without care or competence. To place a student in harm's way because we do not know or do not care is an act far worse than a bungled surgery. Our mistakes will not bleed. Instead, they carry hidden scars whose mean and tragic consequence may not be seen until years have passed and remedy is painful or impossible.

But the beauty and the power of the loving teacher — now that is the greatest instrument for good in our society. All that I am or ever will be, I can attribute to the opportunity provided for me in the public schools and colleges of this nation — and to the men and women who cared for me there. To first-grade teacher Mrs. Oglesby, who taught my dad, my brother, and me. To Mrs. Miller, who caught Mack Rice and me fighting at recess and wore us both out with a splendid switch she kept in the cloak room. To Clint Walker, whose loving discipline launched me into a lifelong love of music. To "Bill" Osteen, who showed me what took place in the "office" when he caught me and Billy Platt throwing erasers in the Latin classroom. To Henry Reeves, who never published a paper in his life but taught me most of the college mathematics I mastered. To Bert Nothern, who lifted my vision from the commonplace. To John Richardson, who pulled me from the comfortable places in life in order to experience the thrill of daring. To those colleagues, students, friends, and members of my family who continue to teach me loving lessons.

This, then, is a story of teaching. It has a simple and single motive — to elevate and celebrate the call to teaching. It is written for the interest and pleasure of those who teach and for others — parents and civic leaders — who care about teaching.

ONE
Acts of Teaching

Take fast hold of instruction; let her not go:
Keep her; for she is thy life.

Proverbs 4:13

Walnut Grove is a quiet, rural hamlet nestled among the cotton and soybean fields of West Tennessee. On a Sunday morning cars and pickup trucks pass, carrying folks to the Cumberland Presbyterian Church, centered among several modest homes strung along the country road running out of Garland. Swaybacked barns bask in the morning sun, looking tired from their years of use. And not far away is a white frame country store and a large metal garage with four John Deere tractors clustered in front.

There is no trace of the one-room school that was the educational center of this community in 1926. It was in this school that 19-year-old Miss Ardell Wiseman took her first teaching post after graduating from the two-year program at West Tennessee State Normal School, now Memphis State University. Miss Ardell, as she was called, taught all eight grades to 15 children in that one-room school.

Ten miles away in Covington, the county seat, the school board — then as today — wrestled with the thorny educational issues of 1926. And in distant Nashville and Washington, D.C., state and national government bodies deliberated over education policy issues. These issues, however, seemed distant and of lesser moment compared to the challenge posed to Miss Ardell on one of the early days of her teaching career.

Noting her small frame of just under five feet and her tender age of 19, the older boys decided to test the mettle of their new teacher. During morning recess, they fetched a fresh "meadow muffin" from a nearby pasture and slipped it into five-year-old Harvey's desk. The heat from the wood stove enhanced the aromatic qualities of the cow

1

manure, disrupting Harvey's concentration on his lesson. It also was becoming apparent to the other children that the smell pervading the classroom was something more than the aroma from unwashed bodies.

When he could stand it no longer, Harvey approached Miss Ardell with some trepidation to tell her what had transpired, while the older boys snickered and waited to see what would happen next. What transpired next was an unorthodox but vigorous application of the basal reader, an application certainly not intended by its author, to the posterior of the meadow muffin culprits, whom little Harvey had fingered.

That evening Miss Ardell consulted her father, Lafayette Wiseman, on other disciplinary options not covered in her normal school preparation — options that offered promise of harnessing the lively spirits in her diverse classroom. One of these options included the placement of a large nail in the schoolroom wall about five feet off the floor. Students anticipating other shenanigans did so only after considering what it would be like to be hung from their overall straps on this large nail for an appropriate reflective period.

Having established her authority, Miss Ardell settled down to a good year of productive work. I don't know what happened to Miss Ardell's pupils. But I can tell you this: Miss Ardell, my mother, is now 84 years old, and I don't give her any sass. This may be the only written record of her pedagogical style; but the strength of her caring and courage lives in me, my sister, and thousands of lives she has touched. She was my teacher as well — teaching the power of discipline, independence, and persistence.

This morning I manage a few moments away from the office to compose these opening reflections. *Sesame Street* is over; and my four-year-old daughter, Sara Love, comes bouncing into the study. I can see hiding in those mischievous blue eyes, freckled face, and auburn locks a little person who falls heir to the determination and strength of Miss Ardell. Will she want to be a teacher?

Teachers joining the profession today have missed one of the most exciting and tumultuous eras in American education. Beginning with the social and educational changes wrought by *Brown* vs. *Board of Education* in 1954 and the Soviet's launch of Sputnik in 1957 on through the critical reports of the Eighties calling for reform and restructuring of our schools, those who labored in our classrooms have lived through a period of great ferment.

In the decade of the Eighties alone, we have been inundated with a tide of critical studies and reports unparalleled in the history of

American education. A short list includes *Education on Trial* (1985), *A Nation at Risk* (1983), *Meeting the Need for Quality* (1983), *A Place Called School* (1984), *The Paideia Proposal* (1981), and *Free to Teach* (1983).

Americans excel at criticism. From barbershop to boardroom, our national penchant for criticism flourishes. The late Texas congressman Sam Rayburn once remarked that any jackass can kick a barn down, implying that a little more in the way of intelligence and imagination is required to be constructive compared to being critical. Nevertheless, Americans love having a go at their politicians, their professors, and assorted other targets including their schools. Stanford professor Elliot Eisner (1982) observes that:

> To appraise the schools and not to find them wanting is, it seems, a tacit admission that one lacks standards. It is far easier, at least as far as these institutions are concerned, to criticize rather than praise. (p. 4)

Concluding a 40-year career of teaching at every level, Elizabeth Hunter (1985) reflects on the recent wave of criticism with these words:

> The schools are too lenient, too lax; they indulge, pamper, and coddle. No, no — the schools are too confining, too rigid; they lack joy.
>
> The school curriculum is frivolous; too little emphasis is placed on writing, numbers, and reading; the hard work that learning requires is ignored. No, no — the school curriculum neglects thinking and favors dull memorization; it stresses conformity and skirts controversial ideas.
>
> Teachers don't discipline as they should; they don't teach sound moral values; they expect too little from students; they don't care. No, no — teachers are too strict; they are unloving; they fail to take account of their pupils' backgrounds; they don't care.
>
> The critics have been at it for a long time now. Whether they speak from an intellectual, a humanistic, or a back-to-basics stance, since the 1940s, when I entered the field, they have been saying that education is just no damn good. (p. 221)

John Goodlad in his landmark study, *A Place Called School* (1984), has these comments about our penchant for criticism:

> When it comes to education and schooling, we Americans want it all. . . . We have, it seems, extraordinary faith in edu-

cation and grandiose expectations for schools. We expect schools to teach the fundamentals, expose students to the world's knowledge, socialize them into our ways of governing and conducting economic affairs, develop their individual talents, and "civilize" them. . . . Yet successive waves of disaffection for schooling concentrate almost exclusively on the small piece of academic shoreline we measure with achievement tests. . . . The relevance and significance of most of what goes on in schools — all that is not included in achievement measures — depend on one's perspective. For a majority of people (i.e., non-parents and parents whose children are not in school), whether schools are satisfying places for the students who attend them is largely irrelevant or of only passing concern. . . . They want schools to contribute to an efficient work force, provide employees who can read, graduate a steady stream of qualified applicants to universities, keep pace with schools in countries where we sell or hope to sell goods, and so on. As measures of school performance, standardized test scores fit comfortably with other measures of our assumed well-being, such as the gross national product (GNP) and the Dow-Jones averages. A drop in scores calls for a hardnosed dose of discipline and fundamentals in the schools. (p. 468)

What, then, do we need to strengthen our schools and colleges in this nation? An extra dose of discipline, elimination of tenure, more time on the fundamentals, deletion of curricular frills, merit pay, more pay, tuition vouchers, less regulation? And what is the response to this barrage of criticism from those who labor in classrooms each day?

First, I think we can rejoice that our schools and colleges have at least been successful in teaching our graduates to be critical. When one is searching for an anchor in an angry sea, this is one performance goal that we have served well. The performance evidence is before us in books, reports, TV documentaries, and newspaper editorials.

Second, I think we may be grateful that more responsible critics recognize that assessing the performance of our nation's schools and colleges is a complex matter that must take account of dramatic social and economic changes. If we looked only at the international economic trends, the movement of women into other professions, the press for equitable and just treatment of minorities in our society, and changes in family structure, we would find more than enough reasons to account for staggering changes in our schools.

4

Third, we must hold accountable any teacher or administrator who would let even one high school or college senior be awarded a diploma or degree that is empty of meaning. Whatever social or economic changes have taken place — and they have been dramatic — no one says we have to give away diplomas or degrees. When any graduate exits our doors without having mastered basic skills, the public has a right to an accounting. The pay may be low and the classrooms hot, the principal may be a tyrant or the college president a decision coward, the student may be trying hard or just marking time — whatever the circumstances, they cannot become excuses for failing to hold students to the highest standards and expecting the best their talent can deliver. The integrity of a credential should reflect our standards, our ethics, our commitment, and our love for students.

Fourth, we must avoid the bitterness that can invade our hearts when society criticizes an enterprise to which we have committed our lives, even though the financial rewards are often meager. We did not enter the teaching profession with the expectation of lavish financial rewards. Nevertheless, it takes a stout spirit not to be troubled when one of your students graduates in a field where the starting salary is significantly more than yours after 20 years on the job, or when collecting garbage pays more than the starting salary for a beginning teacher. We must not give way, however, to a defeatist attitude that takes away our dignity and our devotion; nor should we bend over and invite critics to kick us further. Classrooms, laboratories, playing fields, studios, workshops, and rehearsal halls — these are sites of a precious work. Let us celebrate the nobility of that work and rejoice that teaching is the most completely constructive and positive force in our nation.

Finally, I think we can look for seeds of renewal even in these critical reports. The evidence of that can be seen in the variety of initiatives now being taken by many states. And the evidence also can be seen in the change in public attitudes toward schools. The 1990 annual Gallup Poll reported in the September 1990 issue of *Phi Delta Kappan* indicates that 41% of respondents gave schools in their own communities an A or B rating, up considerably from the 1983 rating of only 31%.

I recently participated in a modest way in the growing school/business alliance movement. Prior to the opening day of school, I joined other Chamber of Commerce members in taking new teachers to lunch, a way of expressing our interest in and appreciation for the work these teachers would be doing. My luncheon group included four young persons starting their teaching careers. Were their qualifications and morale low, as suggested by some of the national reports? I don't think so. Their conversation reflected bright spirits full of optimism. Each of them wanted to be a teacher. They did not enter the field as an afterthought or on a rebound after having failed in some other field. Most of them were honoring teachers in their lives by entering a work in which they could repay that investment.

As these four young teachers move into the classrooms of my city, this I also know: Many of my professional friends in other fields would become mental basket cases if they faced the same environment and challenge these beginning teachers will face tomorrow — a 100-degree classroom in a difficult section of this city, a classroom filled with 25 or more young spirits of every conceivable talent, motivation, and home background. Compared to the place of labor of these new teachers, the work surroundings of the attorney and the accountant, the physician and the psychologist are congenial indeed. And the challenges of closing a mortgage transaction, auditing a set of books, prescribing medication for infected tonsils, or calming an anxious spouse are simple tasks — intellectually, emotionally, physically — compared to the complexity of the tasks facing these new teachers.

Let me close this discussion about the work of teachers with an illustration taken from Pat Conroy's *The Water Is Wide* (1972) (later made into the film *Conrack*, starring Jon Voigt).

Conroy took his first teaching assignment on the South Carolina coastal island of Yamacraw, where he faced the formidable task of educating young black children from impoverished backgrounds. As with any artist teacher, he chose unusual and diverse methods to gain his students' interest and motivate their learning. Who would expect to find, however, the strains of Beethoven's Fifth Symphony issuing from the windows of the wooden-frame schoolhouse on Yamacraw Island? Conroy chose 20 of the most impressive titles in the classical music literature and taught his boys and girls to recognize every one. This is his report of what he next did with critics and cynics who came to visit his work on the island.

> When I started bringing an influx of visitors in the spring, curious people who heard about the island and came basically to pity, to commiserate, and to poke around, it gave me and the kids almost Satanic pleasure to flip on the record player,

6

challenge an unsuspecting guest to a contest in classical music, then let the well-drilled students maul them. Oh, the joy. To see the misty-eyed whites who had flagellated themselves with visions of worm-eaten cretins and deprived idiots trounced in a head-on collision of wits was a banquet to be savored again and again. On the way home, riding through the green marshes, I would explain to the shell shocked visitors that the children felt that Strauss was overrated, you know, old chap, a little too mawkish and sugary. On the other hand, they felt that Brahms was not getting his due with the general public. He had written some fine stuff that had remained unknown to the common run of listeners. Those were good and satisfying days. (pp. 12-13)

To Touch a Life Forever

Teachers save us from the poverty of the commonplace. The purpose of teaching is to promote and to facilitate learning. The acts of teaching are these:

To inform and inspire
To discipline and discomfort
To evaluate and encourage

Here is my 1953 high school annual from Millington Central High School. I am looking at the picture of Kathleen Tennant. For three years, I learned from her algebra, geometry, and trigonometry. And then I went off to Memphis State College. There I was taught college algebra and calculus by Henry Reeves. He did not have a doctoral degree, and he did not have a showman personality. To my knowledge he never published a scholarly article. What he did have was the rare and potent skill of making complex mathematical concepts understandable. These were two important acts of teaching, the acts of Kathleen Tennant and Henry Reeves. They were acts that informed me of the power of analytical skills and cultivated those skills in my life. They were acts for which I remain grateful to this day.

Archie Dykes was at one time a high school principal and country school superintendent. A graduate of Tennessee schools and colleges, he went on to become chancellor of the University of Tennessee at Martin, the University of Tennessee at Knoxville, and finally the University of Kansas. He also served as president and chief executive officer of Security Benefit Life Insurance Company of Kansas. Along the path of a brilliant career, Archie Dykes spent a period of time teaching in an advanced graduate center in Memphis, where I earned 15 graduate hours under his tutelage.

Professionally alive in every sense of the word, Archie Dykes was an active and published scholar and competent administrative practitioner. The acquisition and application of ideas for the improvement of schools was a matter of constant devotion in his life. One could not stand next to the man without feeling the inadequacy of one's own knowledge. If he suggested a book for my reading, I would have it in hand before the sun went down. This was a magnificent act of teaching, an act of inspiration. It was an act that carried me through my doctoral work and set values in place that still form the foundation for my own work.

How I got to doctoral study in the first place may be traced to another act of teaching. Bert Nothern still teaches at Memphis State University. Bert Nothern did one thing for me for which I will always remain indebted. I grew up thinking a doctoral degree was something you needed to practice medicine. It never occurred to me that I should aspire to that degree. But while working on my master's degree and taking a statistics course with Bert Nothern, he took me aside and encouraged me to think about pursuing doctoral work. That was a powerful act of teaching — an act of encouragement — that set my life on a new course. What a difference those few moments in his office made in my future. I hope that Bert Nothern takes pleasure in that investment, and that my professional life honors his investment.

I remember the name of every teacher who taught me in elementary and secondary school. Mrs. Miller was my second-grade teacher. She lived in an unassuming frame house just a block from the school. I occasionally mowed her yard and ran errands for her. I did these things because I respected her. And the reason I respected her is because she caught Mack Rice and me fighting during recess and took advantage of the short pants we were wearing to apply a switch to our bare legs.

In the last 40 years, Ralph Hale has probably produced more musicians in the city of Memphis than all the music educators in that city combined. My first memory of Ralph Hale goes back to the late 1940s when I descended the steps of Melody Music Shop in downtown Memphis to take my place in one of the glass-enclosed cubicles for private lessons on the E-flat mellophone. My memory of Mr. Hale was one of a highly competent but somewhat ascetic man. Some years later I again encountered Ralph Hale when I played first

French horn in the Memphis State College Concert Band, where he was on temporary assignment as director. He spent most of his life as director of bands for Christian Brothers High School in Memphis.

Mr. Hale was a demanding director with high standards for his music and his musicians. He gave compliments infrequently. A compliment from Ralph Hale was an event to be prized for years. I remember playing a spring concert with a guest artist, a baritone player from the U.S. Navy Band. Most of us in the band thought we had played well. When we took our chairs in the rehearsal hall the day after the concert, we expected at least a modest note of appreciation from Mr. Hale. He, however, had a different agenda and plunged stony faced into the rehearsal hour.

This was too much for a few of us. During a break in the rehearsal, several of us asked him what he thought of the concert. He responded with a litany of its shortcomings, including some mention of "woofy tones" emerging from the horn section. Having always been afflicted with a bad case of "hoof-in-mouth" disease, I ventured a risky question: "Mr. Hale, you hardly ever compliment us. How do you expect to get our best effort when you don't compliment us?" He ended the discussion and the rehearsal with this response: "Well, Grady, when you do something that's worth complimenting, you may be sure that recognition will be forthcoming."

This act of teaching had a deflating effect on my ego and my musical aspirations that day. But his words were actually an act of discipline. They lifted our standards from the commonplace and put them on a plane that required some reaching. Ralph Hale is a friend of mine and a friend of mind. I remain grateful for the voice of this teacher in my life.

John Richardson is retired. He is a formidable man who gave his entire life to schools and colleges in Tennessee. He served as a teacher, a principal, state board staff member, graduate dean, and college president. He is a man with a bountiful heart and absolute integrity.

While teaching physics at the U.S. Naval Air Technical Training Center in Memphis during the mid 1960s, I worked on my master's degree at Memphis State in the evenings, weekends, and summers. I was happy in my teaching assignment. But John Richardson pulled me from that role and launched me on an administrative career at Memphis State. This was a discomforting act of teaching. He called me from the familiar to the unknown, from a pleasurable present

9

to an uncertain future. This act of teaching was one of the finest moments in my life.

Ralph Hale, Bert Nothern, Archie Dykes, Kathleen Tenant, Henry Reeves, John Richardson — their acts of teaching characterized able minds, stalwart hearts, and loving spirits. The greatest act of teaching is to expect the best each talent can deliver. The greatest pleasure of teaching is to see talent unfold. The life of the master teacher is an unselfish investment in the dignity and potential of students, a life that honors all that is good and noble. Some of our students will test and disappoint us, and some will escape the error of our judgment of their talent. We will grieve for the former and rejoice for the latter.

References

Adler, Mortimer J. *The Paideia Proposal: An Educational Manifesto*. New York: Macmillan, 1982.

America's Competitive Challenge: The Need for a National Response. A Report to the President of the United States from the Business Higher Education Forum. Washington, D.C.: Business Higher Education Forum, April 1983.

Boyer, Ernest L. *High School: A Report on Secondary Education in America*. New York: Harper & Row, 1983.

Conroy, Pat. *The Water Is Wide*. Boston: Houghton Mifflin, 1972.

Eisner, Elliot W. *Cognition and Curriculum: A Basis for Deciding What to Teach*. New York: Longman, 1982.

Elam, Stanley M. "The 22nd Annual Gallup Poll of the Public's Attitudes Toward the Public Schools." *Phi Delta Kappan* (September 1990).

Felt, Marilyn Clayton. *Improving Our Schools: Thirty-Three Studies that Inform Local Action*. Newton, Mass.: Educational Development Center, 1985.

Goodlad, John I. *A Place Called School*. New York: McGraw-Hill, 1984.

Goodlad, John I. "A Study of Schooling: Some Findings and Hypotheses." *Phi Delta Kappan* (March 1983).

Hunter, Elizabeth. "Under Constant Attack: Personal Reflections of a Teacher Educator." *Phi Delta Kappan* (November 1985).

Johnston, William J., ed. *Education on Trial: Strategies for the Future*. San Francisco: Institute for Contemporary Studies, 1985.

Nathan, Joe. *Free to Teach: Achieving Equality and Excellence in Schools*. New York: Pilgrim Press, 1983.

National Commission on Excellence in Education. *A Nation at Risk: The Imperative for Educational Reform. A Report to the Nation and the Secretary of Education*. Washington, D.C.: U.S. Department of Education, April 1983.

Task Force on Higher Education and the Schools. *Meeting the Need for Quality: Action in the South. A Progress Report to the Southern Regional Education Board*. Atlanta, Ga.: Southern Regional Education Board, June 1983.

TWO
A Good Question

When wisdom entereth into thine heart,
and knowledge is pleasant unto thy soul;
discretion shall preserve thee,
understanding shall keep thee.

Proverbs 2:10-11

The recent film, *The Dead Poets' Society*, is instructive for teachers and parents alike. Set in an exclusive Eastern boy's prep school, it concerns the efforts of a young new teacher, played by actor Robin Williams, to lead his young men in a search for life's meaning through the study of poetry. While the teacher works to put wings on the minds and personalities of his students, we also watch the stultifying effect of a stodgy school administration mired in tradition. And the film causes parents to look inward, as we see one young student struggling to free himself from the imprisoning expectations of his status-conscious parents.

The film's climax rewards our patience with the trials of students and teacher, as we see his class of young men find conviction and courage in a thrilling moment of defiance and personal discovery. And we also see that lovely moment of satisfaction that comes to the life of a teacher when he sees many of his students take wing and fly. The pleasures, the tensions, the lessons to be found in this cinematic journey into teaching are replicated in the daily realities of every school in this country.

Ten-year-old Carlyn has Rubenstein-Tabin Syndrome, has suffered two strokes, and has been wetting her pants five to six times a day for the better part of the school year. She attends Alexander Special School in Shreveport, one of the older schools in the city and one relatively unknown — except to those parents who have children among the 120 who attend there.

11

In her first year of teaching, Carlyn's teacher, Christy Webb, remarks: "I spend much of my day in the bathroom just getting my seven children to zip up, button up, and snap up." Little Carlyn has been potty trained two times, only to lose that training following the two strokes. When I visit Christy's classroom, blonde and smiling Carlyn runs over to hug my neck. I hug back. And then I look more closely over this unusual classroom, an educational reality distant from my university setting.

Earlier on the playground, Larry, who is borderline autistic, caught Christy in an unguarded moment while she was watching one of the other children, pulled down his jeans, and loosed a warm stream down her leg. A microcephalic child, Scotty must wear a padded cloth helmet because he keeps falling down when he walks. Roger is a mischievous 10-year-old with cerebral palsy who spoke not a word to Christy for several weeks until he spotted a wasp coming in for a landing in her hair and yelled, "Hey lady, you got a wasp on you!"

After watching Christy at work with her seven special children, I wonder how she summons the energy to keep up with them all day. And then I find that on the weekends Christy tutors a friend's child with Down's Syndrome. What keeps a young teacher going in a classroom with seven young children, each with a different disorder that robs them of a normal future? What is Christy's source of satisfaction?

Down the hall from Christy, 12-year veteran Linda Bond works with 10-year-old Don. Don has an I.Q. of around 135 but is rejected at home, especially by his father. This rejection has produced a severe behavioral difficulty for Don and is stealing from him the potential of a bright mind. Linda also teaches Janie, who comes from a home where she has been the victim of incest, and 11-year-old Michael, whose older brother was just arrested for armed robbery. How can Linda labor each day to nurture some flicker of progress in each of these young lives — only to see them return to a family environment that tears down quicker than love can build? What prevents a naked rage from building in the hearts of those who teach these abandoned and abused children? There are no salaries large enough to keep men and women at this work, although Christy and Linda will be quick to say that improved salaries are important. And they are both grateful for a recent raise made possible by a multimillion-dollar tax referendum recently approved by Caddo Parish voters. No, the answer to what fuels the daily devotion of teachers like Christy Webb and Linda Bond cannot be found in conventional rewards.

It's discovery. And wonder. And curiosity. Teachers are a people who know the quiet but potent power of compassion, who know how a moment of caring can turn a life to a new path, who know that beyond love the next most enriching human emotion is the excitement, that touch of wonder that comes with learning. This is what Christy and Linda are doing — bringing forth moments of discovery through a devotion filled with both expectation and caring.

Even in these children, whose learning horizons are more limited than those most of us see each day, Christy and Linda can see those moments of discovery. After tutoring mildly retarded Shawn on multiplication tables, Christy is finally rewarded by Shawn's excited cry: "Miss Webb, I have the key! I have the key! I have the key!" His disability does not prohibit Shawn from uttering and understanding a phrase of double meaning. Not only has Shawn discovered the key to understanding the multiplication table, he also understands that what he has learned is the key to opening other doors.

Not five miles away, Georgia Lee is teaching a class of advanced students in history at Captain Shreve High School, one of the city's award-winning public high schools under the leadership of principal Sandra McCalla. A walk through the halls reveals the cultural diversity of its 1,600 students and a hint of the challenges faced by teachers in this high school. This walk also reveals a well-maintained plant and disciplined climate that reflect the pride of both students and staff and the hand of a master principal.

I chat with Georgia during her planning period. She is experienced — almost 25 years as a teacher — and proud of her work. Georgia leads her advanced students in a life of discovery as well, although the character of her challenge and the satisfactions derived are of a different order than those of Christy Webb and Linda Bond. An IBM PC screen winks at me from a side of the classroom, where one of Georgia's student teachers is entering student-progress data. A nugget of Georgia's teaching philosophy almost slips by in our conversation before I get it in my notes. She nods toward the IBM PC and comments, "Machines cannot pat a child on the back nor provide Kleenex for tears."

Georgia invests her life in the challenging but lovely variety of personalities who show up in that classroom each day. What keeps Georgia at her work? Can it be the modest salary she earns after more than 20 years of investment? No. It's that inner grin that comes when she lifts one of her students to a moment of discovery. It's that warm feeling that comes when one of her former students drops in to express appreciation for a moment of caring.

Teachers are in the business of breaking the bonds of ignorance and of cultivating curiosity. Teachers are in the business of assaulting conventional wisdom. Teachers are in the business of provoking their students with good questions and having those students in turn frame good questions. Teaching is the business of constructing and using good questions — the instruments of discovery, the instruments of wonder.

The Instrument of Discovery

Years ago I developed an affection for this little poem by James Kavanaugh.

I Wonder*

I wonder if the waves get weary
with the surf and surfers on their backs
Or if the wind is angry when
it throws the rain against my window
I wonder if the mountains are lonely
or only sad?
I wonder if the gulls are sick of eating fish
if the sandpipers get tired of dodging waves.

. . . .

I wonder silly things — like:
Do sandcrabs live in condominiums?

It is human to wonder — to inquire, to search, to probe, to construct questions. Man is a maker of questions — sometimes in play and reflection as with the sandcrab question, sometimes with serious intellectual intent, sometimes with malicious intent.

A college history professor had prepared a stellar lecture for his early class. He entered the lecture hall and began the lesson in his best professorial voice, moving to a vocal fortissimo as he arrived at each important point, dropping back to a mezzo forte and occasional piano as he laid the groundwork for yet another of his conclusions.

Most of the class responded with interest, respectful of the professor's obvious scholarship. Partially hidden in a top tier of seats in

---

*Copyright by James Kavanaugh. Reprinted by permission.

14

the back of the lecture hall rested a young scholar tired from his late-night job at the local Texaco station. Attending to the lecture was no match for the demands of his exhausted body, and our young friend slipped into a twilight state, hoping to be hidden by the waving hands of some 60 other students in the class.

His slumping posture, however, did not escape the sensors of our lecturing professor, offended that even one of his academic sheep was not hanging on every word he uttered. And so our good professor plotted how he might get the attention of our young man and perhaps extract a measure of revenge as well. As he built his lecture to yet another crescendo, he pointed an accusing finger at our slumbering student and asked, "And you, young man, yes, you in seat 45, do you agree with Will Durant's observation that 'virtuous men, like happy nations have no history'?"

Our sleepy scholar slowly stirred from his stupor and proceeded to think about how he might extricate himself from this difficult and potentially embarrassing moment. His response, an old favorite of students, was to use flattery to appeal to the ego of the lecturer: "Well sir, what do you think?" Puffed up to full size, the prof answered in an arrogant tone, "I don't think! I know!" To which the student responded, "Well, I don't think — I know either!"

Think of all the different ways we can use questions, in both positive and negative context:

To put others on the defensive
To stay on the offensive
To stimulate curiosity
To search for truth
To challenge the arrogant
To strengthen the timid
To promote self-reliance
To elicit commitment

Most people feel that when they are asked a question, they have an obligation, even a natural urge, to answer. We are inclined to attempt to answer before we have thought much about whether the question is an appropriate one. Thus we are easily put on the defensive. But we can stay on the offensive by asking a return question.

Wording of questions is an art form, one that can determine the results we get. For those interested in cultivating the art of asking good questions, I commend the book *Asking Questions* (Sudin and Bradburn 1982). I love their opening illustration:

Two priests, a Dominican and a Jesuit, are discussing whether it is a sin to smoke and pray at the same time. After failing to reach a conclusion, each goes off to consult his respective superior. The next week they meet again. The Dominican says, "Well, what did your superior say?" The Jesuit responds, "He said it was all right." "That's funny," the Dominican replies, "my superior said it was a sin." Jesuit: "What did you ask him?" Reply: "I asked if it was all right to smoke while praying." "Oh," says the Jesuit, "I asked my superior if it was all right to pray while smoking."

Experienced survey researchers know the subtleties of questions, not only in their wording but in their timing (when we ask them) and in the order they are asked. Teachers can learn from these experts. Consider the following:

When is it more effective to ask a broad question of the entire class as compared to asking a specific question of a specific student?

When is it appropriate to ask a question to embarrass a student? To challenge a student? To reinforce a student?

How do we avoid asking questions that pose a threat to the student/teacher relationship?

In my own teaching career, I have become increasingly sensitive to the power of questions. In 1961, having just finished a four-year tour as an electronics communications officer with the Air Force, I accepted a position as instructor at the Naval Air Technical Training Center in Memphis. My first chore was to learn a new vocabulary. The floor was a deck. The walls were bulkheads. The door was a hatch. The bathroom was a head. After that, I began to learn about teaching.

I taught two courses in physics and one in technical writing in a year-long curriculum in engineering electronics. My students were naval and marine officers who had come up through the ranks and then were commissioned as Limited Duty Officers. They were capable men and highly motivated.

I remember my first couple of weeks as though it were yesterday. I was sitting behind my desk one afternoon when in sauntered Lt. White, a huge man standing six feet four and about 240 pounds. Waving his recently corrected physics laboratory report in the air, he slapped it down on my desk and asked: "Mr. Bogue, just what the hell is a dangling modifier?" A good question.

Now there are handy definitions in grammar texts of a dangling modifier — a participial phrase used as an adjective modifier but hanging loose with no noun or pronoun nearby to modify. But it soon become clear to me that Lt. White was not really interested in my explanation. He was there to learn physics, not the niceties of English syntax. And he didn't take kindly to an instructor several years his junior nitpicking about his writing. His question caused me to think about such things as tact and a person's dignity. And I began to learn about the power of good questions in teaching and learning.

Years later, when teaching at Memphis State University, I made use of what I learned from Lt. White. In an early morning class I had a young man from Brooklyn studying to be a teacher. I had asked the class to write a 10-page research paper. Matthew turned in a paper that looked as though he had been using William Buckley's dictionary. I was confronted by such words as prescient, oxymoron, pusillanimous, and autochthonous — from a student who had never shown any proclivity for vocabulary pyrotechnics.

What to do? I was reasonably sure that Matthew had not written his paper. But no proof. As any experienced teacher knows, you don't accuse students, you plot against them. So, I invited him over to my office for a cup of coffee and a chat about his paper.

Obviously discomforted but wearing a weak smile, Matthew sat tentatively on the edge of one of my office chairs. "Matthew," I began, "I found your paper really interesting. In fact, I found some expressions in your paper that stretched my vocabulary a bit. For example, what does this word 'oxymoron' on page 3 mean?"

"Let me see that page, Dr. Bogue." I pointed out the word on the page. "Well, I can't remember the meaning of that word right now." And so it went for some half-dozen words throughout the paper. By the end of our conference, he was grinning like a mule eating thistles, and so was I.

"Matthew, did you write this paper?" I asked.

"No, sir."

"Well, who did?"

"My girlfriend helped me."

"Well she should probably get an A," I responded, "But what should we do with you? I could give you an F on the paper, maybe an F in the course. What I really wanted in this assignment was not what your girlfriend knew and thought but what you knew and thought. Someday you are going back to Brooklyn to teach, and some student is going to do to you what you have done to me. How will you handle it?"

Matthew departed the office with the charge to bring me, within the week, a paper he had written. He did. I gave it a C. He graduated. He is now teaching physical education in Brooklyn, doing something that I can't do; and he is doing it well.

A good question can be used to promote self-reliance, to nurture responsibility, to soften the effect of evaluations. We are inclined to the declarative and imperative when evaluating. "Your performance on that last (test, contract, debate, staff presentation, concert) was not up to par!" This may be an accurate assessment, but might we achieve the same purpose with a softer entree: "How do you assess your performance on the last (test, contract, debate, staff presentation, concert)?"

Let me commend Walter Bateman's *Open to Question: The Art of Teaching and Learning by Inquiry* (1990). This is a book that is both provocative and practical. Using a variety of illustrations, Bateman teaches us the power of pause and puzzle and shows us how to lead students on ventures of discovery in such difficult areas as race and religion, science and sociology. He offers a rich repertoire of teaching strategies designed to bring learning excitement in classrooms from kindergarten to college.

In 1951 I was playing first-chair French horn in our small band at Millington Central High School. One afternoon close to the end of rehearsal, we had just finished playing a march that ended without the traditional "stinger" note on which marches usually end. Thinking of the touch football game that Larry, Walter, and I would play right after band practice, I was not paying attention and let loose with a resounding stinger note. My face turned crimson as that lonely note seemed to bounce around the rehearsal hall for eternity. Our band director, Mr. Ditto, leaning over the podium, smile on his face, asked, "Grady, how did you know what note to play on that rest?" It's been 35 years since I played that lonesome note, and I still remember the effect of Mr. Ditto's pointed question.

When we were yet children, we pestered our parents with a torrent of questions — questions of what and why and when and how and where and who. Where does God live? What makes the grass turn green in spring? Where does the sun go at night? The ultimate outcome of teaching is a student empowered by a sustaining curiosity and a sense of wonder. The ultimate joy of teaching is to see a

18

student enraptured by a moment of discovery. And the most potent instrument of discovery, of curiosity, of wonder is a good question. Questions paint a portrait of our life's purpose, express our values, reveal our joy and agony, lay bare our moments of doubt, and open for inspection the content of mind and heart. Our questions enable us to escape the confines of conventional wisdom.

What is the purpose of teaching? A good question!

References

Bateman, Walter L. *Open to Question: The Art of Teaching and Learning by Inquiry.* San Francisco: Jossey-Bass, 1990.

Kavanaugh, James. "I Wonder." In *Will You Be My Friend?* Highland Park, Ill.: Stephen J. Nash, 1990.

Sudin, Seymour, and Bradburn, Norman. *Asking Questions.* San Francisco: Jossey-Bass, 1983.

THREE
A Good School

Every prudent man dealeth with knowledge:
but a fool layeth open his folly.

Proverbs 13:16

"New Schools: U.S. Is Building Some Fine Ones But Is Facing a Shortage." This was the title of an article in the 16 October 1950 issue of *Life* magazine. One of the new schools featured in that article was the Booker T. Washington High School in Shreveport, Louisiana. On a May morning, almost 40 years after the school was featured in the national press, I visited Booker T. Washington High School. I found there several little-heralded but encouraging stories of teaching.

First stop on a visit to any school is The Office. My last visit to The Office in a student capacity was in the same year that Booker T. Washington opened its doors. Mr. "Bill" Osteen, principal at Millington Central High School in my hometown back in Tennessee, had extended the invitation. He had caught Billy Platt and me throwing erasers in Mrs. Harris' first-year Latin class. One of the errant erasers sailed through the open classroom door at the precise moment that Mr. "Bill" was making his early morning rounds. I learned what takes place in The Office that morning and thereafter contained my early morning enthusiasm for eraser chucking.

The principal of Booker T. Washington is Abram Valore. I estimate Abram's height at six feet six and weighing in at 220 pounds. I decided right away that I wanted him as a friend. Teacher, coach, principal, Abram has been an educator for a quarter-century, 25 years invested in the lives of boys and girls in Shreveport.

Friendly but businesslike, Abram is obviously proud of his school and his 850 students. As with most educators, his greatest pleasure comes from seeing pupil growth and achievement. When I ask about aspects of his work that he finds aggravating, he says only that these are leadership challenges that come with the job. As we walk the halls of the school, I recall lines penned by the scientist/educator for whom this school is named. In my home library is Booker T. Washington's *Up From Slavery*, in which I have these lines underscored:

> I will allow no man to drag me down so low as to hate him. . . .
>
> Nor should we permit our grievances to overshadow our opportunities. . . .
>
> Every persecuted individual and race should get much consolation out of that great human law, which is universal and eternal, that merit, no matter under what skin found, is, in the long run, recognized and rewarded. (p. 28)

Abram is optimistic about the opportunities for the predominantly black student body of his school, but indicates they still face the uncertain burdens of prejudice. "If," he says, "you walk through an open door 10 times and are met with prejudicial acts, these experiences teach you to at least approach the open door with caution. Some will not walk through at all after a few such experiences. Then perhaps one day, you walk through the door of opportunity with no ill consequence. You start to feel more relaxed. But just when you are getting comfortable walking through that door, you may be hit again with a prejudicial club. It takes a special kind of courage and persistence to work against the uncertainty of prejudice, never knowing when it will show itself in your life."

Prejudice can rob the human spirit of hope and dignity. It is an enemy of the educated man or woman! In another of life's great paradoxes, however, we find that good can spring from evil. Those who have struggled against the tyranny of prejudice have produced outcomes of great strength and beauty. Writing in *Black Odyssey*, Nathan Huggins describes a "people whose courage was in their refusal to be brutes, in their insistence on holding themselves together, on acting, speaking, and singing as men and women."

The 1950 *Life* article on Booker T. Washington High School featured its curricula in typesetting, auto repair, and bricklaying. Abram tells me that the school even had a laundry. Most of these programs are no longer offered. Washington is now a parish-wide magnet school for computer science. We enter the building housing the equipment and laboratory space. An IBM 4351 hums away, serving terminals from several schools over the parish. A room of IBM personal computers can be found in the lab next door.

Coordinator of the computer science program is Lou Oliver, now in her sixth year. Following her graduation from Tarleton State University in Texas, she moved to Shreveport and worked briefly as a computer programmer but found that work confining and unsatisfying. She sought a teaching position and was assigned to teach mathematics at Washington, eventually assuming responsibility for the newly implemented computer science curriculum.

Lou is proud of her work, her profession, her school, and her students. She is white but also knows about prejudice — not from her black students but from friends who find it unusual that she chooses to teach at Booker T. Washington. "You teach there!" is the incredulous response when Lou tells friends where she works. I get the impression, however, that Lou handles herself well in these exchanges, leaving her friends a little more sensitive and wiser when they ended a conversation with her than when they opened it. Here is a devoted and competent lady doing a good work.

My third story is found in the language lab on the second floor of the "C" wing. Here I find a beautiful lady completing her 13th year at Booker T. Washington. Wanda Brooks teaches French and Spanish. Inspired by the teacher whose position she took, Wanda has completed her bachelor's and master's degree in French and has earned additional graduate hours. She has studied in France several summers so she can bring more than book knowledge to her students. That her knowledge, experience, and devotion pay off is apparent in the record of her students. Several have won prizes in state language competitions, and others have been selected to receive language fellowships in France.

For Wanda, teaching is more than what takes place in her disciplined classroom each day. She continues to press her students to the merit and performance test set by Booker T. Washington. When two of her students win fellowships for summer study in France but cannot afford the costs to go, the Language Club at Washington raises money to send their fellow students abroad. Here is a quiet story of devotion — not a story, however, that finds its way into the policy reports published at the national or regional level, or even in local media coverage.

Is Booker T. Washington a good school? There is a substantial body of research on school effectiveness. A 1986 monograph issued

22

by the U.S. Department of Education titled *What Works* summarizes that research as follows:

> The most important characteristics of effective schools are strong instructional leadership, a safe and orderly climate, schoolwide emphasis on basic skills, high teacher expectations for student achievement, and continuous assessment of pupil progress.

These are qualities whose presence or absence are not difficult to ascertain in any school. And I believe you could find them at Booker T. Washington on the day when I made my visit.

Writing in the April 1990 issue of *Phi Delta Kappan*, Chester Finn says that we are looking at a fundamental change in how we view school effectiveness. The emphasis will be on results and not on the process. What kind of results? The standardized test results for the graduates of Booker T. Washington have been several points below those of other schools in the city, especially the magnet schools and those having a different racial mix. Does school environment and parental involvement make a difference?

Where do these students at Booker T. Washington come from? Let's go over to Pierre Avenue School, a predominantly black elementary school that feeds into Washington. Here teachers work against special home hardships.

A recent graduate of Centenary College in Shreveport, Kathy Fraser is one of America's young heroines. She began her third year of teaching with a kindergarten class of 37 children! Can you believe that? Trying to teach 37 kindergarten children in any school, but especially with children from deprived home backgrounds, is an overwhelming task. Not until mid-year did Kathy teach fewer than 30. On the day of my visit, she had 24 in attendance.

It is a sunny spring afternoon. Her children are lying on their mats sleeping (supposedly) after a romp on the playground. One young fellow lifts his head, looks at me with big friendly eyes, and waves his little hand. I wave back. Another asleep on the mats is a five-year-old who was raped by her stepfather when she was only two. Her mother has lived with a series of men who beat this little girl regularly. Can Kathy compensate for this home climate? She is devoted to trying. Most of the quarter-million folks living in Shreveport have no concept of, and little appreciation for, what Kathy and a thousand others who serve in our classrooms do each day. Is Pierre Avenue Elementary a good school?

23

Let me tell two other stories to accent the complexity of the question of what is a good school. Last week I was invited to give the commencement address at Lakeshore Special School in Shreveport. The commencement here was a celebration quite different from my university's commencement only a week later. Lakeshore is a school for the mentally retarded. About 40 to 50 parents, guardians, and friends gathered in the sweltering school auditorium at Lakeshore to watch the simple ceremonies for a dozen graduates.

Principal John Crockett, a veteran of our parish schools, opened with brief welcoming remarks. Rather than the resonating strains of Elgar's *Pomp and Circumstance March*, the processional here was softly rendered on the flute by Gail Schell, the school's music therapy teacher. The 12 graduates, robed in attractive blue caps and gowns, marched with proud but uncertain steps down the aisle and up the steps to the stage, where they sat in a single row.

Assistant principal Driskill Horton introduced me. I joked a bit about preparing an hour's address, but indicated that because of the heat in the auditorium I would restrict my remarks to only 45 minutes. Following weak but friendly laughter from the audience, I delivered a quick five-minute reflection on the subject of "A Good School."

The graduates, ranging in age from 18 to 22 and with differing degrees of retardation, then marched proudly by to receive their certificates of completion and other awards and trophies for participation in athletic and musical activities. The grins of satisfaction on the faces of these graduates were every bit as big as those I saw the next week on the faces of our university graduates as they received their bachelor's and master's degrees. Is Lakeshore Special a good school?

This question of what makes a good school continues to press on my mind. A week after I had given the commencement address at Lakeshore Special School, I attended the Rotary Club luncheon, where U.S. Senator Bennett Johnston addressed the group on the subject of Louisiana education, particularly the Louisiana School for the Arts and Sciences, a state-funded school for the gifted and talented located on the campus of Northwestern State University. Senator Johnston had been commencement speaker at the school the previous Saturday and was highly complimentary of its quality. Is the Louisiana School for the Arts and Sciences a good school? Senator Johnston believes that it is. Would he and the 300 men listening to him think that Booker T. Washington, Pierre Avenue Elementary, and Lakeshore Special are good schools?

We spend a good bit of time discussing and debating educational quality as if we had a tight grasp on the issues. We engage in heated exchanges that have few common reference points and little useful outcomes, other than the heat. We issue opinions as though they were fact. We arrive at facile conclusions from the narrowest base of information. Shabby data, shadowy standards, and shallow judgments — these furnish no constructive help for schools and colleges. Let's see if we can bring some organization to our thinking about this question of a good school.

Questions of Quality

Is educational quality measurable or is it something vague and ephemeral? Perhaps a little of both. Several years ago I taught a graduate course in which one of my students submitted a final examination, a take-home essay exam, which was totally incoherent. I had been worrying about this student all term because her performance was well below marginal on almost every assignment for the course and now culminated in this disappointing final examination. I could not in good conscience give this student any grade other than an F.

Later, when she and I discussed her poor performance in my office, I remember the anger in my heart — not with this particular student but with each and every person who had allowed her to progress this far in pursuit of a bachelor's degree without setting reasonable expectations for college-level work. These were acts of educational malpractice that cheated this woman from realizing her potential. Here she was in her early thirties, with plenty of intelligence for good work, having been denied the full use of that intelligence because of low expectations — and apparently because of the absence of any meaningful quality-assurance effort.

The primary purpose of any educational quality-assurance effort is to improve, not to punish. Sometime earlier in her academic career, it would have been relatively easy to determine whether this woman could write a grammatically correct sentence, a coherent paragraph, and a short essay that made sense. Just one talent cheated of its potential is one too many for me.

And then there are times when you know the quality is there, but you may not be able to put an exact number on it. Athletics, music, drama, dance — all artistic ventures and performances fall in this category. Those who have seen Baryshnikov dance or heard Leontyne Price sing and Van Cliburn play the piano know that qual-

25

ity is there, though it may evade our more precise calipers of measurement.

In 1973, I played second French horn with the Memphis Symphony, an orchestra that hardly falls in the same class as the Philadelphia or Chicago Symphony or the New York Philharmonic. Yet on this particular Saturday evening, we were playing on a level beyond the individual talents of orchestra members. I remember the thrill as I answered the first horn in a powerful four-note passage in the third movement of Brahm's First Symphony in C Minor, the final piece of the evening. And I can still remember the chills running up and down my spine as the entire orchestra engaged the powerful notes of the fourth movement. I knew, and each member of the orchestra knew, that we were performing at a level of artistry well beyond anything we ever expected. When the last note echoed into the concert hall, the audience rose in a standing ovation. They knew, too — although there was no test, no measuring device, to tell them.

A quality educational climate is one that stretches each talent to the limits of its capacity, that encourages each talent to explore and find those limits. In an American history course I took at Memphis State University more than 35 years ago, our text, which I still have in my library, carried the following quotation by Alexis de Tocqueville on the flyleaf:

> Providence has not created mankind entirely independent or entirely free. It is true that around every man a fatal circle is traced beyond which he cannot pass, but within the wide verge of that circle, he is powerful and free; as it is with man, so with communities. The nations of our time cannot prevent the conditions of men from becoming equal; it depends upon themselves whether the principle of quality is to lead them to servitude or freedom, to knowledge or barbarism, to prosperity or wretchedness.

Now that's a solid call on the purpose of quality assurance.

In writing about quality assurance in the profit sector, Philip B. Crosby suggests that quality should be defined as "conformance to requirements." His book, *Quality Without Tears* (1984), offers helpful and constructive views on the definition and development of quality. David Garvin, another writer about quality in the profit sector, states in his book, *Managing Quality* (1988), that multiple factors are involved in determining quality. There are many parallels between the profit sector and the service sector, such as schools, when it comes to questions of quality. It seems to me that any discussion about quality assurance or quality assessment must engage the following five questions:

1. Is quality in limited supply? Can only a few students and a few schools possess it?
2. Is quality to be defined by a single performance indicator or does it require a cluster of factors to describe the richness of personal and institutional behavior?
3. How shall we determine quality? Who selects the appropriate standard of performance, and who decides who will make the judgments?
4. What is the purpose of our quality-assurance efforts? Is our primary motive one of improvement or accountability?
5. How shall we recognize and nurture diversity in human achievement?

What quality standards do we expect of Mikhail Baryshnikov, Leontyne Price, Van Cliburn, Jonas Salk, and Bo Jackson? And what of poets and pilots, musicians and managers, engineers and educators, accountants and artists, bakers and bankers, philosophers and plumbers, maids and mayors, lawyers and linemen — what standards do we expect from such a diversity of talents?

No book in my library has meant more to me than John Gardner's little volume, *Excellence*, which I commend to every parent, educator, and civic leader interested in the question of quality in our society. Here is perhaps the most quoted and remembered passage from that book:

> The society which scorns excellence in plumbing because plumbing is an humble activity and tolerates shoddiness in philosophy because it is an exalted activity will have neither good plumbing nor good philosophy. Neither its pipes nor its theories will hold water. (p. 86)

A Quest for Quality

A quest for quality causes us to ask serious questions about educational outcomes, about educational ends. And when we ask questions about educational ends, we are forced to engage a range of questions about educational beginnings — questions of meaning and mission. Thus, ventures into questions of educational quality are renewing experiences — exercises in discovery that can bring learning and excitement and pleasure to educators and others. Here are a few closing notes on our quest for quality.

Reject the notion of limited supply. Americans often have the idea that to have first-rate schools and colleges there must be a larger cluster of second- and third-rate colleges and schools. Ridiculous. They really don't believe what John Gardner said — that it is possible, even essential, to expect first-rate performance of every man and woman, every organization, and every institution.

I join Gardner in the conviction that if we want a first-class, quality society — whether in education, the arts, health, or business — we will not get it by expecting a few to be first-class and the remainder to be second- or third-class. We need to respect diversity of mission and purpose but to expect first-class performance within that mission, be it educating plumbers or philosophers.

There are big schools and big colleges. There are smaller schools and smaller colleges. And questions of quality are independent of their size. Why should any school or college keep its doors open unless it can provide quality performance that is related to its mission. There can be no justification or excuse for educational mediocrity — which in my definition is asking less than the best that each talent can deliver.

Promote public disclosure of performance results. Educators are understandably uncomfortable about public disclosure of student and institutional performance data. And for good reason: the media and critics of the schools are prone to race off with limited data and limited thought, leaping to unwarranted conclusions. Nevertheless, there is a compelling case for public disclosure of performance results.

Almost two decades ago, Leon Lessinger, former U.S. Associate Commissioner of Education, commented in his book, *Every Kid a Winner: Accountability in Education* (1970):

> In financial matters, we require a business or a public agency to open its books to an independent auditor, instead of assuring us of its own honesty and fiscal competence. Why should we require any less with regard to educational results? . . . Provision for detailed public auditing of educational results will bolster educators' professional credentials. . . . Professionalism, in other words, goes hand in hand with accountability, with clear-cut proof of performance. (p. 10)

Now we ought not be too sanguine that such an independent auditing will guarantee anything more for American education than for

American business. We know of corporations that publish slick annual reports, with auditor certification included, that are still engaged in shoddy business or about to enter bankruptcy. Indeed, one of the core difficulties is that the auditing firms themselves have been party to the deception. A look at the media reports on the savings and loan scandals over recent months will verify this difficulty.

What can be constructive about public disclosure, however, is that it encourages schools or colleges to define their own goals and performance standards. Thus they can be evaluated on standards they themselves have developed. How one state moved its entire college and university system to just such a quality-assurance system and public disclosure, I have described in *The Enemies of Leadership* (1985). The practice of public disclosure, I am convinced, has more merit than liability in the quest for quality.

Emphasize performance rather than pedigree. One way to make every kid a winner is to emphasize performance rather than pedigree. When I was in junior high and high school, I would catch the bus each Sunday and ride from Millington into Memphis for rehearsals with the Memphis Youth Symphony under the direction of Dr. Henri Minski. I played second chair and then became good enough to pass up the "city" kids and play first chair. At that point my mother thought I was perhaps good enough that she would try to buy me my own French horn. I had been using the school's up to this point.

What kind of horn to buy? There were the prestigious foreign-made horns, the Paxmans from England, the Schmits from Germany, even the Guyer made in Chicago. The city kids had these foreign-made horns, and their advice for me was: If you really want to be a horn player, buy a foreign horn. This was one of my early introductions to questions of pedigree and status.

On my mother's salary, a foreign-made French horn was out of the question. Fortunately, Dr. Minski also worked at Bond Music Store, and he sold us a Conn 6D double French horn for only $500. I didn't appreciate then what a sacrifice my mother made to buy me that horn, but I did make an important discovery. It's not the equipment, it's the talent and discipline that count first. Pedigree may give you an initial start, but it's performance that pays off in the long run.

Talent can and does emerge from many places in our society — from big comprehensive high schools and from the little high schools tucked away in a rural glen, from the research universities and from the people's colleges carrying names like Northeast, Southwest, etc.

The glory of the story is in the surprise when a talent coming from far back in the pack takes first place on performance.

Balance competition and equity. In order to discover and nurture those talents that may emerge from the quiet and hidden corners of our society, we place a high value on access to our schools and colleges. Making public education at every level accessible to boys and girls, men and women is a dramatic, American success story. But we continue to fret and fuss over reconciling access and quality. At the moment we seem to be moving toward more selective admission standards in many of our public colleges and universities, which in the past served as the gateway of opportunity for minorities, women, and immigrants. Now the pendulum swings as society seems to be saying that we have failed to maintain standards, that we are letting too many ill-prepared students into college, students who are taking resources that should go to the adequately prepared.

This dichotomy between competition and equity strikes at the philosophical foundations of our democratic society. Our economic system is built on the constructive force of competition. Competition is the instrument that propels our energies, sharpens our talents, challenges our imagination, and enforces self-discipline. But there are dangers in competition. Unbridled competition can lead to a dog-eat-dog mentality, where selfishness prevails and integrity is sacrificed, where making the short term look good is done at the expense of the future.

On the other hand, an over-emphasis on equality can have equally damaging consequences, where initiative is smothered, where mediocrity is the accepted standard, and any talent is afraid to lift its head above the average. American literature, fiction and nonfiction, is replete with illustrations of both extremes. I commend for your reading Ayn Rand's *Atlas Shrugged* and Robert Heilbroner's *In the Name of Profit* if you want to look at both sides of the issue. The challenge of leadership is to maintain a creative tension that balances competition and equity.

Promote partnerships in learning. The quest for quality requires partnerships that promote a community of caring for our schools and colleges. We first need partnerships with the home and family. A poor home environment is no excuse for educators to abdicate their responsibilities for motivating students, setting high standards, offering quality instruction, monitoring progress, and insisting on the integrity of credentials, be it a high school diploma or a bachelor's

30

degree. Every effort we can take to involve parents in the ownership of our schools is a step in the quest for quality.

The second partnership has to be between schools and colleges and universities. On questions of quality, the public should turn first to the colleges and universities. It is there that our teachers, principals, and superintendents are educated and receive their professional training. Those of us who work at the college and university level have to become committed partners and work in the trenches with our elementary and secondary school colleagues.

The third partnership has to be with schools and the community. A community that cares about its schools cares about its own health. I recently suggested to the superintendent in my city that it might be a good idea to establish advisory panels for each of our 75 schools in the district. These panels, consisting of a representative group of parents and other interested citizens, would work with the principal in defining the school's goals and establishing performance standards. Here is an opportunity to involve several hundred citizens in the life of our schools. No doubt this involvement will complicate the lives of the principals, the superintendent, and the board; but I am convinced it also will strengthen school-community bonds and contribute to the quest for quality.

The Meaning of Quality

It should be clear from the foregoing discussion that there are different definitions of quality:

Quality means reputation.
Quality means high cost.
Quality means selectivity.
Quality means bigness.
Quality means diversity.
Quality means equal access.
Quality means fitness for use.
Quality means goal achievement.
Quality means value added.

Let me close this chapter by proposing a definition of educational quality. I do so knowing that there will be rebuttal from others with different views. So be it. I define educational quality as:

Conformance to mission specification and goal achievement.

31

The first merit of this definition is that it respects diversity of missions and environmental settings. Is the mission and environmental setting for Garfield High School in East Los Angeles (featured in the film *Stand and Deliver*) the same as the Louisiana School for Arts and Sciences cited in this chapter? I think not. Is the mission of the U.S. Air Force Academy the same as my institution, Louisiana State University at Shreveport? I think not.

A second merit of this definition is that it implies specification of mission and goals in operational terms. Schools and colleges would not be allowed to hide behind lofty and fluffy language as a statement of their purpose. Rather, they would have to specify clearly what performance level they expect to be achieved in order for a student to be granted a diploma or degree.

A third merit of the definition is that it assumes that the multiple stakeholders (teachers, administrators, school boards, parents) will be involved in specifying the mission and goals and thus have ownership in them. Once there is agreement on goals, schools and colleges have a basis for judging what they actually achieved.

A fourth merit of the definition is that it requires public disclosure of mission specification and goals. Public disclosure will open the debate on mission or purpose but narrow the debate on performance. It should certainly encourage consensus building on what we want our schools and colleges to achieve.

Finally, the definition requires stakeholders to engage the questions listed on page 27: What indicators will be employed to judge mission and goal achievement? What standards of performance will be accepted as satisfactory? How and when will we make the judgments and who will make them? And most important of all, what are the purposes for obtaining quality-assurance data?

As John Gardner stated in his book *Excellence*:

> Our society cannot achieve greatness unless individuals at many levels of ability accept the need for high standards and strive to achieve those standards within the limits possible for them.

It's time that we go public on what we want our education goals to be and exactly what we mean by standards. This exercise in quality assurance will surely create tensions in school-community relationships. I am convinced, however, that the venture will be a renewing one for school and community, strengthening the partnership and ensuring a successful quest for quality.

So, what is a good school? Are Booker T. Washington High School, Pierre Avenue Elementary School, Lakewood Special School, and Louisiana School for Arts and Sciences good schools? I contend that if they conform to mission specification and goal achievement, then they are good schools.

References

Bloom, Benjamin S. *Human Characteristics and School Learning*. New York: McGraw-Hill, 1976.

Bogue, E. Grady. *The Enemies of Leadership: Lessons for Leaders in Education*. Bloomington, Ind. : Phi Delta Kappa Educational Foundation, 1985.

Crosby, Philip B. *Quality Without Tears*. New York: McGraw-Hill, 1984.

Finn, Chester E., Jr. "The Biggest Reform of All." *Phi Delta Kappan* (April 1990).

Gardner, John W. *Excellence*. New York: Harper & Row, 1961.

Garvin, David A. *Managing Quality*. New York: Free Press, 1988.

Heilbroner, Robert. *In the Name of Profit*. Garden City, N.Y.: Doubleday, 1972.

Huggins, Nathan Irvin. *Black Odyssey*. New York: Vintage, 1977.

Lessinger, Leon. *Every Kid a Winner: Accountability in Education*. Palo Alto, Calif.: Science Research Associates College Division, 1970.

Rand, Ayn. *Atlas Shrugged*. New York: Random House, 1957.

Stand and Deliver. (film) Warner Brothers, 1988.

U.S. Department of Education. *What Works: Research About Teaching and Learning*. Washington, D.C., 1986.

Washington, Booker T. *Up from Slavery*. New York: Heritage Press, 1970.

FOUR
Lessons for Learners

He that walketh with wise men shall be wise;
but a companion of fools shall be destroyed.

Proverbs 13:20

A book of essays titled *What I Have Learned*, published in 1966, includes reflective pieces from such distinguished personalities as Eric Hoffer, Robert Hutchins, R. Buckminster Fuller, Dwight Eisenhower, and many others. The book was worth its purchase for just one line from South African writer Alan Paton, author of the classic *Cry, The Beloved Country*. In his essay Paton states: "[A]ctive loving saves one from a morbid preoccupation with the shortcomings of society and the waywardness of men" (p. 257). If there is anything that constitutes an act of loving, it has to be teaching.

Take Jean Alvarado, a teacher at J.S. Clark Middle School in Shreveport. Here is a loving lady, who also is a "tough cookie." She grew up hard in San Antonio and knows firsthand the value of an education. She has just come from her classes, where she made a six-foot, 14-year-old young man stand in front of the class to give a three-minute oral report. He failed to bring his note cards, as Jean had instructed, and thus forgot part of his report. He stood petrified before the class in complete silence for one minute, but Jean would not let him sit down. That minute was probably the longest this young man will ever experience in his life, but he won't forget the lesson of persistence that Jean was trying to instill.

For Jean, this act of teaching was an act of love, because she knows this young man is going to need oral communication skills in the world in which he will be living. Jean has been cursed by both parents and students, but she holds each of her students to a high performance standard. "If you are a good student, I'll help make you better. If you are a little slow but are willing to work, I'll help you along the way. If you are just lazy, we'll have hell all the way," says Jean Alvarado.

On one side of the desk are good men and women like Jean Alvarado, struggling each day to motivate learning, giving heart and soul to their students, some of whom may not be much interested in learning. Let us look now at the other side of the desk and see what are the responsibilities of the student.

Both teachers and parents have experienced the disappointment of the unmotivated student. Here is how Elspeth Campbell Murphy, a former elementary teacher in South Carolina, expresses that disappointment in a poem from her little book, *Chalkdust: Prayer Meditations for Teachers.*

Prayer for the Unmotivated Child*

Lord, I'm exasperated!
He won't even try.
Children with far less ability
struggle on like determined little tortoises
while the hare sits,
his mind asleep.

Lord, I've tried so hard to rouse him.
I've prodded and threatened and cajoled.
And if there's some incentive I've overlooked,
some method I haven't tried,
Please show me what it is.

But perhaps the time for prodding has passed.
Perhaps the time for decision is here.
And it is a decision only he can make;
To wake himself up
and run the race that is set before him.

Please let him make that decision, Lord,
before it is too late,
and he is left far, far behind. (p. 21)

The simplest of all lessons for students is the decision to take responsibility for their learning. The teacher's helping hands have limited

---

*Copyright by Elspeth Campbell Murphy. Reprinted with permission.

reach, as the little poem above suggests. Learners must extend their hands as well. Let us look then at some lessons that are important on both sides of the school desk.

The Uses of Anxiety

Can you remember that queasy feeling in the pit of your stomach as you entered a classroom for the first time, wondering whether you had the stuff to master new subject matter, weighing how your performance would measure against fellow classmates, questioning whether you would meet the expectations of the teacher? That early moment of isolation and anxiety is a powerful one, and we often have to fight the urge to run away or withdraw. Sometimes, the only force that keeps us there is the raw force of peer pressure.

For some reason, I can't remember many moments like that as a youngster in elementary and junior high school. But I can remember lots of them as I grew older. I wonder if there's a lesson in this. Does our natural sense of wonder and curiosity shut out that anxiety when we are little children? When do we learn to be afraid of learning?

I can still remember the first day of a course in atomic and nuclear physics taught by Ray Tanner at Memphis State College in the mid-Fifties. Ray was later to become a close friend, but my first impression of him was influenced by his glasses. They seemed heavy and thick, suggestive of high intellect and esoteric scientific research. Will he be hard to follow? I wondered. Will his lectures be pitched above my level of understanding? As I glanced around the class of 15, I saw three or four Korean War veterans and a couple of students with glasses just like Ray's. They must be smart, I thought. They look like physicists. And look, they're wearing slide rules on their belts, a sure sign of analytical and intellectual power. Our ranks dropped in the first two weeks from 15 to 10. I stayed with the course, my earlier anxieties notwithstanding. Did the others give up too early? They missed all the fun.

We didn't have much equipment at Memphis State College in those days. Physics faculty today would throw up their hands in despair trying to teach this course with the equipment we had. With the help of two Air Force veterans gifted in electronics and other fabrication skills, we built our own Wilson cloud chamber and cosmic ray scatter detector. And we spent an entire term trying to make the Millikan oil drop experiment work. Staying with that course in physics and with other courses in mathematics prepared me to approach later courses in statistics at the graduate level with confidence. First anxiety, then comes confidence. No risk, no achievement.

Each learner faces different forms of intimidation. I have a modest quantitative talent, so I don't find most new ventures in mathematics and statistics to be formidable. The mysteries of multiple regression analysis and multi-factor analysis of variance did not cause me a furrowed brow, cold sweats, and rapid heart beat. But there are other terrors for me.

The Air Force found one of them. As an ROTC student in 1956, I attended summer camp at Bryan Air Force Base in Texas, a kind of boot camp for ROTC officer aspirants. There I joined 20 other cadets living in one of the tarpaper barracks left over from World War II. The major commanding our unit said that if the termites ever quit holding hands, the whole base would fall down.

Among the physical tests arranged to sort the men from the boys was a controlled jump from a 50-foot tower, sliding down a long cable. The exercise was designed to simulate a parachute jump. Now this exercise might be okay at an amusement park, where folks pay for the thrill. But to insist that I jump off that tower with only a web harness around my waist and a cable of unknown strength between me and a dusty death in the Texas sun was not my idea of fun. The only thing that made me overcome my anxiety was the humiliation of having to crawl back down the ladder and look each of my cadet buddies in the eye, or the strong possibility that the instructor would push me off the tower if I didn't jump of my own volition.

If I had to jump, why not do it the heroic way and go under my own power, I reasoned. In a matter of seconds that seemed like eternity, I jumped, felt the lurch in my midsection as the harness reached the end of its slack, slid down the cable, and managed a reasonably poised landing some 100 yards away. I emerged from my harness with a hint of swagger and began to urge my cadet colleagues to jump, hoping that this show of bravado would distract them from noticing that I had come off the tower with eyes closed and all sphincters in a similar position.

What's the lesson for learners here? It's simply that we all face that moment of uncertainty and fearfulness — that moment of anxiety — when we attempt to learn a new skill or grasp a new idea. Yes, there is the possibility that we might fail. We might give up too soon, thus denying an opportunity to push our mind and spirit to the edge, to grow in ability, confidence, and vision. But the learner who overcomes anxiety becomes heir to new joys. Taking the risk rather than accepting defeat without trial emboldens the learner, quickens the mind and body. Such a learner has practiced the art of adventure.

The Art of Adventure

Overcoming initial anxieties is to practice the art of adventure, the art of risking and daring. No achievement, great or small, no new skill or idea is purchased without some risk. Courage is not the absence of fear. It is the willingness to proceed in the face of that fear — a second lesson for learners.

As I write these words on a late Wednesday evening, I am reminded of how I began my service as chancellor of Louisiana State University at Shreveport. It was the summer of 1980 when my wife, Linda, and I drove across the Mississippi River bridge in Memphis. We had tears in our eyes and uncertainty in our hearts as we left behind the state of Tennessee, our families and friends, and all that was familiar and safe. Crossing that bridge was more than a physical act. It was an act of adventure.

The previous year I had suffered a heart attack at age 43, bringing my race through life to an abrupt and rude halt. The cardiologist told me I had two major blockages in my arteries. As I lay in a bed in Baptist Hospital in Nashville, Tennessee, I remember thinking that I might die any moment, or that perhaps I was destined to be an invalid for the rest of my life, however long that might be. I had never been really sick in my life until that point. Hospitals were places to visit other folks. My doctors advised that treatment would consist of exercise and a somewhat restricted diet — the usual, low sugar, low salt, low fat. And so I did that. I walked and ate lots of bananas, whole wheat bread, Grape-nuts, and fish.

Roughly one year after the first heart attack, I had a second and was immediately taken to surgery. My five-month pregnant wife was told that I had a 50-50 chance of coming out of the surgery, since they proposed to initiate the surgery while I was in the middle of the attack. I didn't have time to act courageous, since they had put me under the anesthetic and I was out while all this conversation was taking place.

I had become a candidate for the chancellor at Louisiana State University in Shreveport about four months after the first heart attack and had made my first visit to the campus in the fall of 1979. As one of the final candidates, I was invited back for a second interview. The second heart attack occurred one week after returning to Nashville from the second interview in Shreveport. I survived the surgery in good order. Not wanting to run from life or to be foolish, I asked surgeon Bobby Frist and internist Roger Jackson what the rules of play were going to be for me. They advised that I could take on any reasonable assignment short of mountain climbing, which they did not advise.

After consulting with my doctors, Louisiana State University System President Martin Woodin and the Board of Supervisors gave me two months to recuperate. The surgery was in early March. On 2 May 1980, I went to Baton Rouge to interview with the board. They sat around a long conference table. Longtime Board of Supervisors member Camille Gravel asked the first question, a question President Woodin had warned me would be forthcoming. "How do you assess your health and its effect on your ability to provide leadership for the university." I responded, "If Bo Schembechler can have by-pass surgery and coach the University of Michigan football team and Menachim Begin can have by-pass surgery and run the state of Israel, I feel I could run the university." I got the job.

They say stress is bad for the heart. Type A folks (I qualify) are supposed to be particularly susceptible. There is lots of stress in a college presidency, but there are many satisfactions, private and professional. In our years in Shreveport, we have had a satisfying family and professional life. We have made new friends, faced new challenges, accomplished new achievements. Could we have known these without practicing the art of adventure, without having crossed that bridge in late June of 1980?

The Advantages of Action

Linda Henderson is principal at Creswell Elementary School in Shreveport. Creswell is one of the older schools in the city, now about 60 years old; but it is clean and inviting to learners. I walk into a kindergarten classroom and encounter the unexpected. Here is a full-size, bright-blue fishing boat occupying the entire end of the room — not exactly the kind of equipment one finds in your everyday kindergarten room. This boat is a "learning center" and is occupied by laughing and learning children on the sunny morning of my visit. I suspect it was not purchased with school equipment money.

The school library is bright and cheerful, with dolls and cuddly stuffed bears peeking over library shelves, sparking children's curiosity to find out what is between the covers of the books directly below. The science room upstairs contains a large planetary display built by the children.

Linda Henderson is an educator who has earned her way. A black principal in a school with mostly white teachers, Linda is respected by her teachers, loved by her children — a lady devoted to her work and competent to do it. She is grateful for the opportunity provided her in the schools of Louisiana and returns that investment now in the love she spends on Creswell Elementary School.

As we walk through the school, we pause at the activity room where a group of children are playing a game of ball. As Linda watches the children play, she tells me she can tell which children are likely to have problems with reading by observing their physical coordination. An interesting connection, one important to our lessons for learners. Reflection and action are partners in the learning process. I want to explore that link further.

Down the hall is the classroom of Lois Wilson, a veteran teacher of 25 years. Lois was cited as an outstanding teacher in the parish in 1974. She shares some of the letters she has received from parents. Here is one from Kay and Eddie Vetter. Eddie is a professor of sociology at Centenary College in Shreveport and a former education staff member for the Chamber of Commerce, a man deeply involved in the civic life of this city. Thus, he and his wife are in a position to appreciate the work of an artist teacher.

Lois tells me about "winter's child," a young girl in one of her earlier classes who came to school in the middle of the winter wearing a tennis shoe on one foot and a sandal on the other. Lois went out and bought this child a pair of shoes with her own money. This is not a story that can be found in any of our national reports on school reform. It is not an unusual story; I have uncovered similar acts of caring in almost every one of the schools I have visited this year. Lois loves her children completely — physically, spiritually, educationally.

But this is a story about knowing and doing. Creswell is an elementary school where mind and hand are at work together. Learning the basic skills, a fundamental mission these years, is enhanced by enriching and complementary activities in music, art, and physical education. Linda Henderson manages her teacher resources so she can afford specialists in these areas, because she knows that action and reflection are reinforcing learning ventures.

40

Physician/researcher James Austin's book, *Chase, Chance, and Creativity* (1977), is an autobiographical and reflective work on the factors associated with the creative impulse, the discovery and construction of new ideas. Although the book focuses primarily on the field of medicine, it has application in many fields. In a section titled "The Varieties of Chance," Austin reaffirms a point we've already considered: the necessity for risk and adventure. He then describes serendipitous ways we encounter opportunity or unexpected good luck.

One way is what Austin labels the Kettering principle, named for Charles Kettering, one of the founders of General Motors. Austin quotes Kettering as follows: "Keep on going and the chances are you will stumble on to something when you are least expecting it. I have never heard of anyone stumbling on something sitting down" (p. 72). Austin then goes on to say, "Chance favors those in motion. Events are brought together to form 'happy accidents' when you diffusely apply your energies in motions that are typically non-specific" (p. 78).

Thus action unites head, heart, and hand in a reinforcing synergism. Principles and relationships become more meaningful when they are put into action. And the abstractions of theory become more concrete as we move from the conceptual level to practice. Moreover, action leads to new associations, which can result in some unexpected turns of good luck.

The writing of this chapter is an illustration of what I have just shared. The book by Austin just cited had slipped from memory. It was still in my library. In fact, I had made some margin annotations on the pages dealing with the varieties of chance. As I sat composing this chapter, Austin's ideas seemed to emerge unsummoned to furnish an illustration for what I was writing.

The linking of learning and doing is a powerful association. I rediscover that power every time I attempt to write. I keep thinking that I will compose this chapter in my mind and then sit down and let the thoughts spill onto the page. But that's not how writing works. There are days when writing would never take place if I waited for inspiration to motivate me. There is something about the physical act of hitting those keys that opens a mental door and my thoughts begin to march across the page. A forgotten illustration or quote springs from memory. One does not learn in the passive mode. You have to be an active participant.

One final note on this business of action. Action also implies persistence in learning. I studied physics in college and picked up good ideas on that first pass. But then I had the opportunity to study physics a second time — this time as a teacher of the subject at the Naval Air Technical Training Center in Memphis. That's where I met Warrant Officer Smith, who turned out to be both my student and my teacher.

Warrant Officer Smith was the prototypical marine — impeccably dressed in his starched uniform, military crew cut, lean physique, and sharp facial features. He had studied a bit of physics and appointed himself as my critic for the course. He caught every mistake I made — every decimal point out of place, every incorrect formula, every sloppy explanation. Each day in that first term of teaching physics was an intellectual and emotional tug of war. I had to keep a special container of Extra Dry deodorant in my desk to contain my overworked sweat glands.

But I held on. I persisted. I taught physics as though I really knew what I was talking about, until Smith pounced on me. Then I went out and studied into the night and came back again. When we arrived at the end of the term, Smith knew more physics than when he started. And I knew a lot more physics than when I started.

The Role of Adversity

Too often in our teaching we stress the arrival and not the journey. In our school and college laboratories, we have students conduct "experiments." They gather data, plot the results, and fit these data to an appropriate mathematical algorithm. But this may not be the most important part of science. The laboratory experience does not tell us about the doubt, the uncertainty that may have rested within the mind of the creator, the failures preceding the success, the rugged persistence necessary to give birth to a scientific discovery, or even the persecution inflicted on some scientists who dared to question the conventional wisdom.

In his marvelous book and TV series, *The Ascent of Man*, Jacob Bronowski tells the story of Galileo, whose investigations confirmed the heliocentric theories of Copernicus concerning the nature of the universe. Here the clash of faith and reason resulted in a momentary defeat of good science. Galileo was brought before the Inquisition by Pope Maffeo Barberini and was tried and found guilty of heresy. At 70 years of age, Galileo was shown the instruments of torture. However, it was not necessary to use them, because Galileo issued his historic confession of error and recanted what he knew to be the truth. But the truth persisted.

Now many school children and budding scientists learn of Galileo's work and its consequences, but few learn of the personal turmoil he experienced at the hands of the Inquisition. Few students will face the hardships of Galileo as they attempt to master new ideas, but they most certainly will encounter adversity in some form.

What constructive role does adversity serve in learning? There are several. Confronting competing ideas serves to test the strength of our knowledge and conviction. How may we claim ownership of any idea, value, or conviction unless we test it against another — in debate, on the playing field, in the courts, and in the classroom? In a small sense the adversarial climate I just described in my physics classroom with Warrant Officer Smith led both of us to learn physics.

Adversity serves another important purpose. It deters arrogance. Yes, we need to express confidence; but occasionally confidence spills over into an overbearing conceit. We begin to think that we know more than we really do. When confidence crosses over into arrogance, it becomes hard, insensitive, and mean. As Whitehead noted in *Adventure of Ideas*, "The folly of intelligent people, clear headed and narrow visioned, has precipitated many catastrophes" (p. 48).

Adversity also teaches the value of mistakes and failure. I don't know anyone who enjoys failing. I know I don't. Failure is a painful and disquieting moment, a threat to our self-concept. But there is a flip side to failure and mistakes. Physician Lewis Thomas comments in *The Medusa and the Snail*:

> Mistakes are at the very base of human thought, embedded there, feeding the structure like root nodules. If we were not provided with the knack of being wrong, we could never get anything useful done. We think our way along by choosing between right and wrong alternatives, and the wrong choices have to be made as frequently as the right ones. We get along this way. We are coded for error. . . . The capacity to leap across mountains of information to land lightly on the wrong side represents the highest of human endowments. (pp. 37-39)

Thomas notes that this capacity for error and mistakes is what keeps humans ahead of computers. Computers, you see, do not have the capacity to make mistakes. Thus we never expect anything very extraordinary or imaginative from them. Only human beings have the capacity to create the novel out of a mess.

The lead story in *Paul Harvey's The Rest of the Story* (Aurandt 1977) is a splendid illustration of my point. John Pemberton was a druggist in Atlanta in the late 1800s who had developed a cough syrup. The story goes that a clerk in the drug store mixed some of the syrup one day for a customer; but instead of using water, he used carbonated water. The result of this mistake was Coca Cola, which we can buy today as Classic Coke, New Coke, Caffeine Free Coke, Diet Coke, and Cherry Coke. A computer never would have made that mistake. Computers will never have any fun and they will never get rich.

It is not in avoiding mistakes but in learning from them that growth occurs. In getting up, dusting ourselves off, putting on a smile, and reflecting on the mistake and what it taught us about ourselves and life, we will grow. We have to live through adversity before we can sense its power for learning. We will not discover that power by giving up.

The Joy of Achievement

Achievement is purchased with a thousand small acts of discipline. I can still remember the inner pleasure I felt when I mastered the notes on my French horn that form the melody for " My Grandfather's Clock." That was in the sixth grade. First I learned to play whole notes, then half notes, then quarter notes, then eighth notes. But the melody became apparent to me only when I put those notes together.

Perhaps someday, I will derive some pleasure from the composition of this essay. Not this day, however. This is a time for writing when the thoughts don't seem to come easy. This is a time for work, for thought, for trying out ideas, for throwing away those that don't seem to fit, for wrestling with the sequence of ideas to make a convincing argument. If I am fortunate, I will practice what I am preaching in this essay and experience the joy of achievement, of producing a publishable piece.

Along with the joy of achievement, there is joy in the journey as well. As Bronowski notes in *The Visionary Eye* (1978):

> For it is not the thing done or made which is beautiful but the doing. If we appreciate the thing, it is because we relive the heady freedom of making it. Beauty is the by-product of interest and pleasure in the choice of action. (p. 34)

And so I sit before my PC on this Labor Day afternoon; my three children are taking an afternoon nap, and my wife, Linda, is enjoying a few moments of well-earned rest. Why am I in the study on this sunny afternoon when there is so much to be done outside? I have a choice and a decision. And, as Bronowski noted, I enjoy the freedom of the decision — a decision to work on this essay, which might inspire and inform others in the future and lead them to become more effective learners, more appreciative of the teachers who call them to that journey.

The Unwanted Lesson

For the most part, I have described in this chapter lessons for learners in situations where the learning is purposeful and the students are willing. But there are other lessons — unwanted lessons hidden in experiences we did not seek and did not want, painful experiences in the journey of life. The value of these unwanted lessons can be fully appreciated only in retrospect. Let me illustrate.

A few years ago I heard Captain Gerald Coffee, U.S. Navy retired, speak at the annual Community Prayer Breakfast in Shreveport. He told of his long years of imprisonment during the Vietnam War. He explained how his religious faith had sustained him during those years of separation from his family and his country. He described how the prisoners learned to communicate with one another through a code they devised using a series of taps for different letters of the alphabet. Thus they were able to send messages by tapping on the walls separating their cells or by using spaced coughs while walking in silence in the exercise yard. By means of this code, prisoners were able to inspire and support one another while in isolation.

It is difficult to express my feelings while listening to this man affirm his faith and his love of country. Tears swelled in my eyes and my stomach knotted up as I listened. The lessons Captain Coffee learned as a prisoner of war make any discomfort I have experienced in my life pale in comparison. Unwanted lessons. They can be as important as those we seek.

Anxiety — first we are uncertain, perhaps even afraid. Adventure — we decide to take the risk, to plunge in and discover new ideas and establish new relationships. Action — we take the new concept or skill learned in the classroom or laboratory and put it to work. Adversity — we are confronted with dissonance and dissent that tests our integrity. Each of these are steps on the way to achievement. Each is a lesson for learners.

References

Aurandt, Paul. *Paul Harvey's The Rest of the Story*. Garden City, N.Y.: Double-day, 1977.

Austin, James H. *Chase, Chance, and Creativity: The Lucky Art of Novelty*. New York: Columbia University Press, 1977.

Bronowski, Jacob. *The Ascent of Man*. Boston: Little, Brown, 1973.

Bronowski, Jacob. *The Visionary Eye: Essays in the Arts, Literature, and Science*. Cambridge, Mass.: MIT Press, 1978.

Murphy, Elspeth Campbell. *Chalkdust: Prayer Meditations for Teachers*. Grand Rapids, Mich.: Baker Book House, 1979.

Paton, Alan. "The Challenge of Fear." In *What I Have Learned: A Saturday Review Book*. New York: Simon and Schuster, 1966.

Thomas, Lewis. *The Medusa and the Snail*. New York: Viking, 1979.

Whitehead, Alfred North. *Adventure of Ideas*. New York: Free Press, 1967.

FIVE
A Need to Know

Whoso loveth instruction loveth knowledge:
but he that hateth reproof is brutish.

Proverbs 12:1

Why does education now look so much like it did 50 or a 100 years ago?

Why can't educators translate research results into practical improvements as engineers, physicians, and farmers do?

With so many years and dollars invested in education research, where are the theories of learning that undergird the practice of teaching as a clinical science?

Is teaching an art or science? Or to put it another way, is there a scientific base to the art of teaching?

What, beyond a mastery of subject matter, do teachers need to know to teach?

It would be hard to find a setting, with or without educators present, in which you could not find passionate debate on all of these questions. In *Entrepreneurship and Innovation* (1985) Peter Drucker points out that "[O]nly now is learning theory beginning to become a factor in our schools. Perhaps the time has come for an entrepreneur to start schools based on what we know about learning, rather than on the old wives' tales about it that have been handed down through the ages" (p. 110). To many, however, it is by no means clear that there is a consensus on the core of knowledge needed for effective teaching, to say nothing of the learning theories alluded to by Drucker.

Among the many education reform reports issued in the Eighties is *Tomorrow's Teachers* (1986). This is a report from the Holmes Group, a consortium of professionals representing some of the largest and most prestigious research universities in the country. It states:

> Efforts to reform the preparation of teachers and the profes-
> sion of teaching, must begin, therefore, with the serious work

of articulating the knowledge base of the profession and developing the means by which it can be imparted. (p. 63)

From this report one might conclude that schools and colleges of education across the nation were doing little more than passing on the old wives' tales suggested by Drucker. One scholar who takes a different position is B. Othanel Smith, who comments in *A Design for a School of Pedagogy* (1980):

Pedagogical practice has made significant progress in this century largely because of the rise and growth of research. Despite this fact, negative attitudes toward pedagogical education are widespread. As we reconsider pedagogical education in the broad scope we are immediately confronted by the claim that there is no adequate knowledge base for such a program. (p. 49)

Smith goes on to outline that knowledge base, which we shall return to momentarily.

A Knowledge Base for Teaching

First, there are confessions we need to offer. The knowledge base for the science of the art of teaching is imperfect and inadequate. Few principles of teaching have been empirically confirmed. Causal connections between teacher behavior and pupil learning are modest in strength and few in number.

However, there are few clinical professions whose history will not reveal a similar condition. It has hardly been 100 years since the largest medical issue facing the nation of France was how to import several million leeches for blood letting, when the domestic supply was exhausted. Quinine was used successfully in the treatment of malaria long before we understood the causal relations involved. It is quite possible that a future perspective might make some of today's surgeries — tonsillectomies, radical mastectomies, and heart by-pass surgery — look rather barbaric. As physician Lewis Thomas recounts in his book *The Youngest Science* (1983), the medical literature of the turn of the century makes horrifying reading today:

Paper after learned paper recounts the benefits of bleeding, cupping, violent purging, the raising of blisters by vesicant ointments, the immersion of the body in either ice water or intolerably hot water, endless lists of botanical abstracts cooked up and mixed together under the influence of nothing more than pure whim; and all these things were drilled into the heads of medical students. (p. 19)

48

As late as the middle of the 1930s, Thomas reports:

> We didn't know much that was really useful, that we could
> do nothing to change the course of the great majority of the
> diseases we were so busy analyzing, that medicine, for all its
> facade as a learned profession, was in real life a profoundly
> ignorant occupation. (p. 29)

The scientific base of the art of medicine is, for the most part,
a development of the past 50 years. And even now, with all the scientific
and technical advances of modern medicine, the manner in which
health care is dispensed can have a deleterious effect on the well-
being of patients. Consider the following incident shared recently
by a physician friend of mine.

An elderly man had been operated on by an orthopedic surgeon
for a fractured hip. Following the surgery, the patient failed to re-
gain consciousness and remained in a comatose state. Given the patient's age, the surgeon and another attending physician were not
optimistic about the patient's recovery. Concerned friends of the patient asked my physician friend to come by and look in on the patient. His diagnosis was that the man had contracted pneumonia with
attendant high fever causing the comatose state — apparently not an
unusual condition in older patients. Treatment for the high fever
brought the patient back to consciousness in short order, producing
what appeared to be a miracle in the eyes of the patient's family.

Science was at work in both instances with this patient. In the former, the narrowness of the surgeon's interest prevented him from seeing other options, whereas science and art were both at work in the
second, more constructive, diagnosis.

As for the profession of law, we were well into the latter half of
this century before the poor of this nation could stand before the bar
with a court-appointed attorney to represent them. It took a prisoner
in a Florida penitentiary (see Anthony Lewis's *Gideon's Trumpet*,
1964) to bring about that change. If we are to break the logjam in
today's courts or reduce the number of frivolous and unnecessary
lawsuits, it is likely that someone other than a lawyer will initiate
the action to achieve those changes.

It took farmers 25 years to accept hybrid corn and equally as long
to accept other scientific advances in the raising of other crops. The
distance between the farming of yesterday and recent advances in
catfish and crayfish farming or the cloning of calf embryos, for example, is long indeed.

Developing an educated human being is far more complex than developing a better breed of corn, cattle, or catfish. Teaching is a normative enterprise. The challenge of educating children and youth is neatly encapsulated by philosopher Harry Broudy in his article, "The Search for a Science of Education" (1976), in which he gives the following hypothetical illustration:

> Suppose, *Mirabile Dictu*, it were announced that a project funded by the Department of Health, Education, and Welfare had discovered a variety of pills that would teach Johnny to read, spell, fill out income tax forms correctly, achieve any SAT score his parents might choose, and adopt any set of wholesome values the school board might specify, including respect for schooling. Here would be a triumph of educational technology that ought to gladden the hearts not only of Johnny's parents but the hard-headed tribes of accountabilists and scientists.
>
> What reception would such an announcement receive? We can conjecture that the first reservations would come from Johnny's parents. First, they would like to know what else will Johnny learn if he takes the pill? Second, who decides which pills Johnny is to be given? Third, when can Johnny go off the pill? The first question comes back to Dewey's observation about the complex effects of any learning experience, the second bares our major concern with social engineering – who watches the engineers? The third is the most crucial of all because Johnny is supposed to become a human being who engineers himself – a subject, not merely a manipulable object.

I still believe that much of the dissatisfaction that Americans have shown toward their schools and their teachers is often related to the mixed anticipations we have for the mission of our schools. I was browsing through Jacques Barzun's classic work, *Teacher in America* (1945), the other day and came across this passage written more than 45 years ago:

> Dissatisfaction is the keynote. Why dissatisfaction? Because Americans believe in Education, because they pay large sums for Education, and because Education does not seem to yield results. At this point one is bound to ask "What results do you expect?"
>
> The replies are staggering. Apparently Education is to do everything that the rest of the world leaves undone. Recall the furor over American history. Under new and better management that subject was to produce patriots – nothing less. An

influential critic, head of a large university, wants Education to generate a classless society; another asks that Education root out racial intolerance (in the third or ninth grade, I wonder?); still another requires that college courses be designed to improve labor relations. One man, otherwise sane, thinks the solution of the housing problem has bogged down – in the schools; and another proposes to make the future householders happily married couples – through schools.

Then there are the hundreds of specialists in endless "vocations" who want Education to run out practical engineers, affable hotel keepers, and finished literary artists. (pp. 6-7)

Sound familiar?

The theme of this chapter is simple and direct: that there is a reasonably well-developed knowledge basis for the art of teaching. Failure to recognize and master that knowledge base can put our students in harm's way and be far more damaging in human consequence than the worst surgeon working with a rusty scalpel. In a few simple illustrations I hope to reveal something of what that knowledge base embraces and perhaps a bit about the limits of the base as well.

Let me lead into my discussion by posing these questions:

1. What are – should be – the goals of teaching? When and under what circumstances are we teaching for the mastery of facts, developing understandings, honing skills, and nurturing sound judgment?

2. What do we know about means for motivating pupil performance and about how and when to use these motivational techniques? Does the knowledge of a motivational technique necessarily suggest how to apply it?

3. What do we need to know about the developmental stages and special needs of those to be taught? For example, at what age can we reasonably expect young children to be ready for reading? Having established a mean age for reading readiness, how much diversity can we expect to find around that mean?

4. What might be the most effective instructional delivery mode for the goal we have in mind? Should we employ the conventional lecture, a seminar or case-study approach, some variant of programmed learning, or a computer-managed approach?

5. What means will we employ to find out whether students have learned what we want them to learn? What are the respective merits of essay and objective examinations? Can a simple question asked by a teacher be perceived as an instrument of threat as well as an instrument of pedagogical skill?

51

Perhaps one of the reasons so many otherwise informed and educated adults take the position that teaching is a simple combination of subject matter mastery with a healthy dose of common sense thrown in is that most of their experience is with adults. They have seldom thought to ask the questions above. I have a litmus test for these critics.

Teachers or supervisors of adults can assume a good chunk of shared knowledge and background experience. But take those college professors, state senators, or bank vice presidents and put them in a class with 25 kindergartners in a crowded classroom on a 90-degree day and see how long it will take them to change their mind about whether there is anything to know about teaching. These young children will not sit passively and listen to a dull lecture and accept that as teaching. More important, they will not learn.

Another challenge to the art of teaching is to take the science, however limited it may be, and put it to work. In his book *The Scientific Basis of the Art of Teaching* (1986), N.L. Gage has a section titled "Knowledge That vs. Knowledge How." In it he points out that studies suggest that reinforcement strengthens the development of behavior. Thus, when my son Barrett comes home from school and we do homework together, I am busy with all kinds of small reinforcers: a pat on the back, a quick hug, the words "Good work, son." However, knowing how to use reinforcement — what reinforcers and with what frequency — is a part of both science and art.

Gage elaborates on this point with these comments: "We may know that criticism in very small amounts may be good for the achievement of more academically oriented pupils, but not know how to limit our criticism to those small amounts for that kind of pupil" (p. 44).

Moreover, we need to know who the "academically oriented" pupil is. This is a question of definition, which B. Othanel Smith says is one of four kinds of pedagogical knowledge we need for the work of teaching. In the sciences, we use a variety of mathematical and verbal expressions to provide operational definitions of terms, definitions that facilitate communication and replication of scientific work in different settings. Thus the definition of the term "force" in physics is mathematically and operationally defined as the product of mass times acceleration, or $F = ma$. But in teaching there are thousands of words and terms whose definitions often lack precise definition. The lack of precise definitions is, in fact, an enormous problem in education. Some perspective is useful here, however.

In his *Hard Gains in the Soft Sciences* (1981) N.L. Gage offers an interesting commentary on the importance of small gains, even in the hard sciences. He cites first a medical study, costing $20 million, which tested the effect of a drug on the survival rate of men who had already had one heart attack. The results indicated that there was a 2.5% difference in mortality after 30 months between two groups of men, half of whom had been given the drug propanol and half a placebo; that is, 7% of the patients receiving the drug treatment died and 9.5% of patients receiving the placebo treatment died, a difference of 2.5%. Gage cites another $250 million study on a drug treatment for lowering cholesterol. Of the men receiving a drug and diet treatment, 8.1% had a heart attack; of those receiving a placebo treatment, 9.8% had a heart attack, a difference of only 1.7%. Yet this study was hailed in both the medical literature and the popular press as one that would profoundly affect the practice of medicine. What is it, in our national psyche, that leads us to accept such small, but statistically significant, differences as of major importance in medicine and trivial in teaching? No, pedagogical research is not the only field where we can make progress on what appear to be modest results.

It might be appropriate to note here that our current state of knowledge about students and schools (achievement of students, average scores of different age groups and graduates, and comparisons on state, national, and international levels) is based on principles of tests and measurement that have been available to us for less than a century, with the major developments in the last 25 years or so.

And so we can have principles − another form of pedagogical knowledge, according to Smith − and still lack useful prescriptions for how to put these principles to work. For example, knowing that immediate feedback strengthens learning is a useful and well-documented principle. This principle at least tells us that we should return exam papers with comments and would argue against the practice of some teachers (especially at the college and adult level) of not returning papers and exams at all.

This same principle suggests still a third form of pedagogical knowledge, that of values. For example, as a teacher I hold to the value that any work produced by one of my students − whether a paper, test, or other product − is to be returned as soon as possible with comments, praise, corrections, questions, or suggestions for improvement. This value is built on the aforementioned principle of reinforcement and is the beginning of a philosophy of teaching. Many a college student, however, can tell you of teachers who do not hold to that value. Is it because they know nothing of the principle of reinforcement or because they cannot translate that principle into a prescription for practice? Whatever the answer, the failure to provide feedback diminishes student learning and motivation.

Smith identifies another form of pedagogical knowledge: facts. It is important, for example, for the fourth-grade teacher to know the fact that one of her pupils is reading at the first-grade level or for a college counselor to know that an entering freshman has made a score of 14 on the ACT college aptitude examination.

And then there are distinctions between "academic" knowledge and "clinical" knowledge, according to Smith. For example, in teacher education programs, academic knowledge includes some familiarity with the history and philosophy of American schools. Is it useful for the new teacher to know that tax-supported high schools in this nation are a development of the last century, or that as late as the 1950s only about half of the white students and one-fourth of the black students graduated from high school? With all the discussion about "literacy" and "illiteracy," is it important for teachers to know how the terms are defined, to know that our operational definition of literacy has changed over the years from simply being able to sign your name to the level of skill expected from an eighth-grade education? Even while we are criticizing our schools and our teachers, the standard of what it means to be literate has been rising.

Academic knowledge about schooling and learning comes to us from history, philosophy, sociology, and psychology. Clinical knowledge remains imperfect and inadequate. But we are not without useful data here. Kathy Slaney was my son's kindergarten teacher. I don't know where she acquired this piece of clinical knowledge, but you can see it when she works with the children. When she talks to a child, she bends at the knees and places herself on a level with the child. This is a symbolic body movement as well, conveying intimacy and a friendly relationship.

How teachers handle relationships is a vital part of clinical knowledge. Dr. James P. Comer, a child psychiatrist turned education reformer, speaks to this point:

> All of the educational reform talk and reports of the past few years ignore child development and relationship issues. And yet when you ask school teachers and administrators what is wrong, they say, "a lack of respect, discipline, and motivation" — all relationship issues. When you ask high school students why they

didn't do well in school, or left, the most often heard complaint is: "The teachers don't care." — a relationship issue. The question I heard from school staff about parents is: "How do you get parents to participate in the school program?" — a relationship issue.

In B. Othanel Smith's *A Design for a School of Pedagogy*, he suggests five domains of knowledge for teaching (pp. 93-94). They are:

1. Diagnosis of student readiness, ability;
2. Planning of course goals, experiences, content;
3. Managing of learning resources, time, facilities, student conduct;
4. Communication through lectures, discussion, questions, praise, reprimands; and
5. Evaluation of student performance and achievement.

I would like to conclude this chapter with examples of the knowledge base in two of the above domains (planning and evaluation) and illustrate how ignorance of them can result in harm to the learner and inefficiency in the teaching-learning process.

One of the first questions facing the artist teacher is planning the instructional objectives for a particular course, unit, or daily lesson. What, for example, do we expect pupils to have mastered by the time they complete the first grade? What do we expect mathematics majors to have mastered by the time they have completed the bachelor's degree? What do we expect students to have mastered by the completion of a unit on the physics of light? What do we expect students to have mastered by the completion of a statistics lesson on measures of central tendency?

Perhaps the most helpful source for planning educational objectives is Benjamin Bloom's *Taxonomy of Educational Objectives: Handbook I: Cognitive Domain* (1956). This seminal work by Bloom and his associates is a source of pedagogical knowledge that serves teachers when planning courses, units, or daily lessons.

The taxonomy of the cognitive domain is a hierarchy of intellectual skills from the simple to the most complex. The six levels of the hierarchy are: Knowledge, Comprehension, Application, Analysis, Synthesis, and Evaluation. Now here is a pedagogical construct that enlivens the art of teaching. For the pedestrian teacher, instruction is simply a business of dishing out facts and figures, and evaluation amounts to little more than the regurgitation of those facts and

55

figures. This exchange defines the teaching-learning process at the most elementary level of practice.

The artist teacher, however, uses the taxonomy to plan objectives that require students to use all levels of intellectual functioning, from the simplest to the most complex. To illustrate I shall use the teaching of grammar and writing as an example of how the taxonomy can be used in planning educational objectives.

Knowledge is defined as those objectives that emphasize learning and recalling facts, terminology, classifications, or principles. For example, I may expect the student to learn the parts of speech.

Comprehension involves the understanding of what has been presented and encompasses the skills of interpretation, translation, or extrapolation. Here I may expect students to recall what they know about parts of speech and use it to explain how the parts of speech function in a sentence or to construct sentences that demonstrate understanding.

Application involves the ability to put ideas and concepts to work in solving problems. At this point, I might ask students to write a basic business letter, a resumé, a short essay, or a book review.

Analysis involves the ability to separate a problem or issue into component parts and to show relationships; for example, to distinguish fact from opinion in a piece of writing. Here I might give students a newspaper advertisement for a new product or a political advertisement and ask them to analyze the appeal or argument used in these materials.

Synthesis is the ability to take facts and opinions and put them together to make a logical and coherent statement or argument. An assignment involving synthesis might be to ask students to review the factors surrounding a controversial issue at school and to write an editorial for the school newspaper.

Evaluation is the ability to make judgments of merit or worth, to discriminate. Here we might have students evaluate an essay. This would involve setting up criteria for the evaluation, such as grammatical correctness, effective use of supporting materials such as illustration, quotes, statistics, logic of argument, and effectiveness of transition.

Bloom's taxonomy is such a useful instrument. It not only makes us think about the cognitive levels when planning educational objectives, it gives us a useful instrument for developing those objectives. Finally, it furnishes a link to the final and perhaps most critical part of the teaching process: evaluating learning, which is my second illustration of pedagogical knowledge.

The purpose of evaluation is to determine whether our students have learned what we have attempted to teach. Unlike medicine, we don't have any "noninvasive" means of doing this. We don't have any sensor devices that can tell whether a student knows what a verb is, can write a decent sentence, or critique an essay. There has to be a demonstration of performance, the design of which calls for another area of pedagogical knowledge.

Will we use a written examination or some form of practical test? If a written exam, will we use an essay, multiple choice, or true-false items? Will we use a norm-referenced or criterion-referenced approach? Will we construct the test so that it contains both criterion and diagnostic items? The diagnostic items can help the teacher find out why students might have difficulty learning or understanding a particular concept. What are the probabilities that a student's final score may not be related to his knowledge but to the construction of the test?

There is a continuum of ignorance with regard to educational evaluation and measurement. At one end of the continuum are those who believe that testing instruments provide a mathematical certainty for making educational judgments. A student's test score becomes an absolute, providing an unequivocal guide for decision. It is disturbing when a teacher fails to realize that a grade of 79 on a final examination is not a fixed entity but one fraught with error from several sources, including the way in which the test was constructed and administered. At the other end of the continuum are those who feel that tests are virtually useless.

How will I go about grading my examination? Back to the question of what does a score of 79 mean. Here are some of the typical thoughts of teachers constructing examinations:

> If all the students get the test item right, how can I have a distribution of grades?
> If the items are too easy, everybody will get them right.
> Gee, I'm not allowed to give everybody an A no matter how well they perform. It just isn't done.
> What about the student who tried hard but just didn't quite make the criterion score? Surely you don't expect me to fail him.
> What about the student who does ten times more than I asked for? Surely I can't give him the same grade as someone who just barely squeaked through.

Here we go again. We are deep into questions of philosophy, which is where the artist teacher ought to be.

Years ago I taught a course in statistics and research design. In my Saturday morning class was a young lady for whom statistics was not an easy experience. After every class, she would follow me to the office to tell me how hard she was working. She also let me know that this was the last course she needed for graduation and dropped the hint that a passing grade was absolutely essential for her to graduate.

One Saturday morning after class, I invited her to sit down with a cup of coffee for an exchange that went something like this:

"Laurie, you are an exceptional tennis player, are you not?" (She had won the city women's tennis championship the previous year).

"Well, Dr. Bogue, I suppose I have some talent for tennis."

"Laurie, if I came to study tennis with you and practiced hitting the ball over the net for eight hours every day for five months, and if at the end of that time I still could not get the ball in the opposing court, would you give me a passing grade?"

"Well, I don't think so."

"Okay. I'm not going to give you a passing grade in this statistics course just because you say you are working hard every week. Now you can pass this course. You just need to concentrate on the assignments rather than spending all your time telling me how hard you are working."

Laurie did pass that course. She may not have been the most brilliant student of statistics, but she was bright enough and disciplined enough to do the job. I knew this and realized that my evaluation of her would require more than a set of test scores in my grade book. It took a personal confrontation to get Laurie headed on the road to success. What I didn't tell her was that the probability of her mastering the mysteries of analysis of variance was far greater than my mastering the skill of serving an ace on the tennis court.

Summing Up

I have touched on several topics related to the question, "What does a teacher need to know in order to teach?" However, I have hardly begun to engage all the substantive topics that can and should constitute the knowledge base for pedagogy. What, for example, does the middle school teacher need to know about the psychology of adolescence? How does one determine the most effective instructional delivery method for a survey economics course for college sopho-mores? What developmental characteristics determine readiness for reading?

Structure and sequence, intuition and intellect, readiness and rein-forcement, motivation and measurement — yes, there is a substan-tive knowledge base for teaching. That knowledge base may be imperfect and incomplete, but only the ignorant and arrogant will reject the good ideas already available — ideas that would lift them from the level of the amateur to that of artist teacher, ideas that will keep them from putting students in harm's way.

References

Barzun, Jacques. *Teacher in America*. Boston: Little, Brown, 1945.

Bloom, Benjamin S., et al. *Taxonomy of Educational Objectives: Handbook I: Cognitive Domain*. New York: David McKay, 1956.

Broudy, Harry S. "The Search for a Science of Education." *Phi Delta Kappan* (September 1976).

Comer, James P. *Maggie's American Dream*. New York: New American Library, 1988.

Drucker, Peter. *Entrepreneurship and Innovation*. New York: Harper & Row, 1985.

Gage, N.L. *Hard Gains in the Soft Sciences*. Bloomington, Ind.: Phi Delta Kappa, 1981.

Gage, N.L. *The Scientific Basis of the Art of Teaching*. New York: Teachers College Press, 1986.

The Holmes Group. *Tomorrow's Teachers*. East Lansing, Mich., April 1986.

Lewis, Anthony. *Gideon's Trumpet*. New York: Random House, 1964.

Smith, B. Othanel. *A Design for a School of Pedagogy*. Washington, D.C.: U.S. Department of Education, 1980.

Thomas, Lewis. *The Youngest Science: Notes of a Medicine-Watcher*. New York: Viking, 1983.

SIX
A Servant Profession

How much better is it to get wisdom than gold!
And to get understanding rather to be chosen than silver.

Proverbs 16:16

Is teaching a profession? I like to think so. And I see that others do, too. One of the sections in the Holmes Group report cited earlier, *Tomorrow's Teachers* (1986), is titled "An Agenda for Improving a Profession." Here's another monograph titled *The Making of a Profession*, penned by Albert Shanker (1985), long-time president of the American Federation of Teachers. Remember the Gilbert Highet volume, *The Immortal Profession*, which I cited in the preface? I like that combination of modifier and noun. And I like the combination of words B. Othanel Smith uses to conclude his monograph, *A Design for a School of Pedagogy*: "Think of teaching as a noble profession."

And here's another impressive contemporary work, *A Nation Prepared: Teachers for the 21st Century* (Carnegie Task Force on Teaching as a Profession 1986). The dignified blue cover on this report wraps around a number of important recommendations presented by 14 of this nation's eminent educators. In the executive summary are these recommendations:

> Create a National Board for Professional Teaching Standards, organized with a regional and state membership structure, to establish high standards for what teachers need to know and be able to do, and to certify teachers who meet that standard.
>
> Restructure schools to provide a professional environment for teaching, freeing them to decide how best to meet state and local goals for children while holding them accountable for student progress.
>
> Require a bachelor's degree in the arts and sciences as a prerequisite for the professional study of teaching.

60

Develop a new professional curriculum in graduate schools of education leading to a Master in Teaching degree, based on systematic knowledge of teaching and including internships and residencies in the schools.

Mobilize the nation's resources to prepare minority youngsters for teaching careers.

Relate incentives for teaching to school-wide student performance, and provide schools with the technology, services, and staff essential to teacher productivity.

Make teachers' salaries and career opportunities competitive with those in other professions. (pp. 2-3)

Now this is a brace of actions I like in both spirit and substance. However, the ink was hardly dry on this May 1986 Carnegie report when a critique appeared in the September 1986 issue of *World And I Magazine*, titled "A Botched Attempt at Education Reform" by Myron Lieberman.

Lieberman opens with the comment that "Educational reform reports have been a growth industry in the United States in recent years" (p. 86). One need only glance back through the citations in these essays to affirm that conclusion. He then goes on to argue that some of the report's recommendations are built on faulty thinking. On the issue of over-regulation, for example, he takes a shot at one of the task force members, Bill Honig, California's State Superintendent of Public Instruction, indicating that it is not so much teachers that are over-regulated as it is school boards and school administrators. He selects a couple of choice examples of bureaucracy from California to make his point.

Regarding the recommendation of collective accountability, Lieberman asks this question: "Suppose, for example, that educational achievement declines instead of increases. Do we fire all the teachers?" "Who will hold the teachers accountable?" he asks. He then speculates that implementation of the report's recommendations would essentially have unions running the schools. He warms to his role as critic with this indictment: "Some task force recommendations appear to have been drafted by Hans Christian Andersen," implying a fairy-tale quality to the report, and concludes his critique with this line: "If anything is certain about this report, it is that all of its major recommendations will not be implemented. For this, we can all be grateful" (p. 92).

For another perspective on the issue of teacher professionalism, Albert Shanker, in *The Making of a Profession* (1985), makes this observation:

At one time we were viewed as quite powerless, given flowers for our lapels on Teacher Recognition Day, patted on the head. Then along came this adversarial procedure known as collective bargaining. The pendulum has swung, and virtually no one now views teachers as being patable on the head — the pooch barks and even bites. We tend to be viewed today as though we are acting only in our own self interest. Teachers want better salaries and small classes so their lives can be made easier. (The public rarely considers that what we want may be good for children.) That image is standing in the way of our achieving professional status. We must act on behalf of our clients and be perceived as acting that way. (p. 12)

Shanker goes on to point out, correctly I believe, that if teacher unions continue to focus their energies primarily on adversarial activity and collective negotiations, teachers will not achieve professional recognition and reward. He suggests the following five ways to promote professionalism:

1. Develop a national teacher examination consisting of three parts: a subject matter examination, an examination of pedagogical knowledge, and an internship of one to three years.
2. Expand choice of school options for parents, students, and teachers. Noting that "Children are the only clients who are perceived as the captives of the professional who deals with them," Shanker emphasizes the need for loosening up school bureaucracies to allow more choice.
3. Establish a professional teacher board for these purposes: to develop standards and ethics for the profession, to handle complaints from parents, to evaluate textbooks, and to investigate questions of teacher incompetence.
4. Establish a different kind of career ladder, the highest level of which would be a small cadre of career/professional teachers who are paid very attractive salaries. These professional teachers would in turn supervise bright interns, as suggested below.
5. Restructure the delivery of education to include the increased use of technology (computers, videocassettes, etc.) and the possible use of large numbers of bright but transient members of the teaching force, young men and women who might serve only three to five years.

Still another view on teacher professionalism is Paul Woodring's opinion piece appearing in the 23 November 1986 issue of the *Chroni-*

cle of Higher Education, titled "School Teaching Cannot be Considered a Profession as Long as Its Entrance Standards Remain so Low." His opening remarks are instructive:

> The noun "profession" has always troubled lexicographers. The adjective "professional" is even vaguer. We speak of professional athletes, professional actors, and even of professional prostitutes and criminals. About all we are implying is that such people work for money and are good at what they do. Realtors, morticians, and stockbrokers are among the many others who now claim professional status. In our society of status-seeking, such striving is understandable, but according that recognition dilutes the concept of professionalism.

Woodring suggests that a profession requires a commitment that goes beyond monetary gain, that it be based on an organized and scientific knowledge base, that it be dedicated to improvement of humankind, and that it requires rigorous standards of selection and education. It is the last of these that Woodring believes to be the central problem for teaching to be accepted as a profession.

What Woodring does not acknowledge, however, is that standards for admission to teacher education programs have been tightened all across the country in the form of minimum grade points, tests of basic skills, and other criteria. It would be difficult to find any teacher education institution not now requiring a cluster of standards for both admission to and exit from the teacher preparation program, including a passing score on the National Teacher Examination and some kind of personal assessment through an interview.

Another recommendation for upgrading the profession, which has caused considerable controversy, is that teacher education be moved from the current four-year undergraduate program to a five-year professional degree culminating in a Master of Teaching, a Master of Pedagogy, or a Master of Arts in Teaching degree. This recommendation in found in the previously cited *A Nation Prepared: Teachers for the 21st Century*, the Holmes Group report *Tomorrow's Teachers*, and also in a report from the Education Commission of the States titled *What Next? More Leverage for Teachers* (Green 1986).

There are dissenting voices, however. A 1986 bulletin from the Southern Regional Education Board (SREB), an influential research and policy body, states its position as follows:

> The SREB position is that until the undergraduate curriculum is revitalized, and truly represents college level work be-

ginning with the first freshman course for credit, it is premature to give up on the four-year program as the typical route for preparing teachers. (p. 1)

The SREB goes on to justify its position with these words:

> Although manpower forecasts of shortages or surpluses sow their own seeds of adjustments as students react to them, there is likely to be a shortage of teachers in the coming years. Such a time does not provide the most opportune moment for a switch to lengthen the required education to enter teaching. (p. 6)

Another opposition view comes from John King, Distinguished Visiting Professor of Education at the University of South Carolina, in a debate appearing in the September/October 1986 issue of *Change Magazine*. King calls the Holmes proposal dangerous:

> It is dangerous because it would injure and hamper rather than support and assist the public and private colleges now producing 80 percent of the teachers for the country. It is dangerous because it ignores many of the root causes of poor morale and ineffectiveness among teachers and schools in the U.S. It is dangerous because it offers simplistic answers to many serious, complex questions faced by teacher-education institutions. It is dangerous because it would place the control of teacher education in the hands of the very universities that have shown the least support and concern for it during the past twenty years. It is dangerous because the public school teacher is considered a second-rate career choice on nearly all the campuses of the existing and proposed Holmes Group. Indeed the Group's own colleges of education occupy a lowly status role on nearly all of their home campuses. (p. 34)

While King makes his arguments with great stylistic force, they have little to do with the merit of the five-year professional preparation program for teachers. There is no question but that private institutions and those institutions associated with the American Association of State Colleges and Universities (AASCU) have produced most of the teachers in the nation. And I think there is little question that some of the nation's research universities have neglected their teacher education programs and even, as King suggests, look down their academic noses at these programs. Nevertheless, many of the institutions in the vanguard of the five-year graduate-level programs are the very ones championed by King. For example, an AASCU institution such as Memphis State University graduated its first class of MAT students in the summer of 1986.

While the current debate on extending the teacher preparation program to the graduate level is heated, it is hardly a new issue. In the early 1950s, Yale University began offering the Master of Arts in Teaching degree; and it continues to be offered at many institutions across the country. In the 1980 monograph, *A Design for a School of Pedagogy* cited earlier, B. Othanel Smith essentially proposed a pre-professional curriculum for both elementary and secondary education majors, which would serve as an undergraduate foundation for admission to a Master of Pedagogy program composed of two years of study beyond the bachelor's degree, including an intensive internship/clinical experience in the schools.

I like the five-year model for teacher preparation. I like it for these simple reasons. I believe requiring an undergraduate degree in an arts and science discipline builds intellectual strength into the teacher preparation program, and this in turn would foster status for the profession. Second, almost all fifth-year proposals assume an intensive academic year of clinical work under the tutelage of a master teacher. If practicing teachers are united on any point about their preparation programs, it is on the value of the student teaching experience. A frequently heard complaint, however, is that these experiences too often put the novice in settings that are artificial — in the better schools and classrooms rather than in some of the more difficult schools where they may have to teach. A more intensive and rigorous clinical year might allow students to experience a greater diversity of clinical environments. A third argument has to do with the "academic knowledge" referred to in Chapter Five. For example, the psychology of learning, human development, and tests and measurements are going to be more meaningful when they are studied in the context of application in classroom settings.

Finally, in human service professions, maturity helps. Here is a new teacher, 21 or 22 years old and fresh from her preparation program, being thrust into a high school classroom. Among her students are a few on drugs, a few who don't care, a few abused at home, a few with limited ability, a few with ability but not challenged in previous grades, a few interested only in putting in time till they can earn money to buy a used car. This young teacher must cope with apathy, arrogance, and aggressiveness. She could use a little more time under the close supervision of a master teacher. Perhaps that one or two years suggested by Smith and others would make the difference in this young teacher's decision to stay in the profession.

What about the issue of whether increasing the length of the teacher preparation program would affect the supply of teachers? Isn't it foolhardy to make the preparation program longer and more rigorous when the country is facing a projected teacher shortage? Such an attitude would be intolerable in other professions. In earlier years, when faced with what we perceived to be a national shortage of physicians, we didn't reduce the preparation time for physicians; we built additional medical schools — at a cost of millions of dollars. Only now are we beginning to see an easing of the demand in medicine and dentistry. We did not, however, reduce admission standards or the preparation time for physicians!

On the matter of teacher salaries, I think we should not be overly optimistic that they will rise dramatically in response to this increase in preparation level. Individuals drawn to teaching will continue to be those who find intrinsic satisfaction in their work to be more important than compensation levels. On the other hand, I do not discount the attractive and retentive power of a good salary. It would be interesting to see what kind of talent would be attracted if teacher's average starting salaries were suddenly doubled.

How often I hear that phrase, "We can't solve our educational problems by just throwing money at them." Maybe so. But consider the observation of Anne C. Lewis, writing in the January 1990 issue of the *Phi Delta Kappan* on comparisons of U.S. and Japanese schools: "The salaries paid beginning teachers [in Japan] are higher than those for entry-level engineers, and teachers' salaries remain higher throughout their careers than those of engineers and other white-collar workers."

Still another informing perspective on teaching as a profession is that of Roger Soder, writing in *The Moral Dimensions of Teaching* (Goodlad, Soder, and Sirotnik 1990):

> Doctors did not attain their preeminent position merely because they claimed to be altruistic or because they claimed to possess a scientific body of knowledge or because they claimed to "police their own" or because it became more difficult to get into medical schools or because medical school training became more extensive. Rather, doctors achieved their preeminence and gained mastery of their profession (or, more appropriately, the occupation) because of a combination of economic and social factors. (p. 63)

Soder then goes on to outline a series of factors, many external to the practice of medicine, which combined to elevate the profession of medicine. These factors included, for example, the linking of scientific medicine to medical training, the increased specialization of medicine, and the entry of powerful support groups related to hospitals, research centers, etc. Soder suggests six "tests" that will determine whether teaching will emerge as a profession:

1. A new technology of schooling would have to emerge with results clearly more effective than current practice.
2. Training of teachers would have to be linked to this new technology, with accredited and relatively standardized courses of study over the nation.
3. The public would have to believe that only those practitioners who have completed the training program should be admitted to teaching.
4. Schooling would have to become a deeply felt and specifically supported high priority of our society.
5. There would have to be no compelling alternative sources of schooling.
6. There would have to be more bifurcation of authority with teachers gaining clear command of decisions related to the application of the new technology, and school administrators would have less authority.

Soder concludes that teaching cannot take the same route to increased professionalization that medicine did.

In a subsequent chapter in *The Moral Dimensions of Teaching*, Barry Bull argues that:

> The full professionalization of teaching the young either as a public office or as a licensed practice is not, however, justified. An office or a practice is professionalized when the selection of office holders or the making of licensing decisions is accomplished by the members of the profession themselves, rather than by those who are directly or indirectly accountable to the citizens of a democratic polity. There is not, in the first place, a sufficient difference between what the public expects and what it has a right to expect (as there may be in law, for example) to justify professionalizing the selection of those who hold the office of schoolteacher. Nor is the knowledge basis of teaching competence secure enough to justify the professionalization of teacher licensure. (p. 117)

Bull's argument on the nature of public and licensed professions in a democratic society is provocative, as is his conclusion. I want to think some more about this view on the nature of teaching as a profession. For a long while, I have felt that lay voices should be present on the licensure boards for physicians and attorneys. I'm not ready to argue against the important role of the laity on matters of school purpose and performance, but I am ready to conclude that too many teacher amateurs can, as I have already noted, take their students and their schools in harm's way because of ignorance and arrogance.

So, we have different ways of looking at teaching as a profession. Some still view teaching as a craft. See, for example, Kenneth Eble's *The Craft of Teaching*. Some are unable to reconcile teacher unions with professional status — although many will admit *sotto voce* that the American Medical Association has on more than one occasion engaged in activities that make it look like a union, and there have been incidents of physicians going on strike. It would appear, however, that there is a clear movement to strengthen the professional status of teaching.

Reforming the Laity-Professional Partnership

Surveys of public confidence in the professions do not present a pretty picture, and the likelihood of future tensions between laity and professionals is high. One could argue that, like the poor, the errant professional is always with us. However, just one such errant professional is too many! Just one teacher who fails to expect the best of his students, just one physician who regards patients as objects with a dollar sign affixed, just one attorney who has forsaken justice to live in a web of duplicity and deceit, just one clergyman who has forgotten that God's calling is to be a servant, just one professional who has become so accustomed to looking down on people that he has forgotten what satisfaction there is in looking up to them — just one is too many!

Earlier, I remarked that education is a profession that historically has been accountable to the people. Here is what I mean. Laypersons are involved in almost every major policy related to education in this country. Through local and state boards of education and through college boards of trustees, they have a powerful voice in such decisions as who is admitted, who is retained, and who is graduated. In addition, laypersons serve on boards that establish policies on such matters as qualifications for admission to teacher preparation programs and requirements for credentialing and licensure. Finally, the laity is involved in deciding how much money will be spent for schools in the form of tax referendums, bond proposals, and legislative appropriations each year.

Professionals still retain control of the teacher preparation curriculum. But if there is any doubt that the laity is voicing its concern and exercising its right of participation, one has only to examine recent state legislation and regulations regarding teacher education. Perhaps there are exceptions, but I am unaware of any licensure board for the other professions (law, medicine, engineering, nursing) that provides opportunity for lay voices to be heard. In my view, the principle of accountability to the people through lay oversight of professional policy and practice should be extended to other professions. If the professions are truly interested in nurturing greater public confidence, they will actively seek lay involvement in the basic policy questions of licensure, access to service, cost of service, and effectiveness of service.

On the question of effectiveness of service, one could have good fun with any of the professions. Let me use education for an illustration. The technical task of assessing educational effectiveness is complex but not impossible. We have seen great strides in assessment and evaluation in schools and colleges over the past 50 years. Indeed, it is the very existence of assessment methods that now allow laypersons to judge effectiveness, because performance data are now available for public scrutiny.

What I think educators need to do now is to involve laypersons in the definition and assessment of effectiveness. They could begin at any level from elementary school to college. Let parents and other citizens join with the faculty to decide how the effectiveness of a particular school or college will be judged. I can predict that several good things will happen very quickly.

First, everyone will discover that it is impossible to assess effectiveness without first determining what the school should be doing and what it hopes to achieve — a question of goals, if you will. Thus, a question of ends forces a question of beginnings. Second, everyone will soon discover the need for multiple measures or indicators of educational effectiveness, because no single indicator is sufficient to measure effectiveness. Third, everyone will discover that there are some exciting concepts from other professional fields that have application in education. For example, lawyers will be pleased to learn that the advocacy-jury model is being applied with some frequency to judge the effectiveness of educational practice and policy. Finally, everyone will discover the complexity of assessment in education, that it is not quite the same as quality control in manufacturing tin cans. It will be a renewing adventure for both laity and professionals.

Moving to other professions such as law and medicine, how shall we decide what the quality of health and justice is in our community, state, and nation? And a corollary question: How is effectiveness in health and justice related to expenditure? The active solicitation of laity to participate in such basic professional policy questions as licensure, access, and cost effectiveness is a constructive − if uncomfortable − force in recovering public confidence.

Renewing Ethical Force

It is a sobering fact that the number of years spent getting an education does not necessarily produce good men and women. When a high school teacher is indicted for selling drugs to students, we have an ethical issue. When a college faculty member gives students a grade of B with virtually no investment of effort or demonstration of knowledge gained, we have an ethical issue. When a highly trained surgeon treats his patient as an object, we have an ethical issue. When an attorney knows the law but violates what he has sworn to uphold, we have an ethical issue. There are no courses in arrogance or altruism in our professional schools, yet they both are learned somewhere along the line.

In *U.S. News and World Report* (10 November 1980) Johns Hopkins University President Steven Muller comments that universities are turning out "highly skilled barbarians." In an equally sharp commentary appearing in the *CASE Currents* (September 1979), Norman Cousins writes, "[W]e're producing barracudas, people who sharpen their teeth on one another, people who ignore the vital fact that their success in their profession will depend not only on their ability to do things, but also on their ability to understand what human beings are all about and to make a contribution to their age." Barbarians and barracudas! Harsh terms for university and professional school graduates. Perhaps this kind of public commentary reveals why we are having so much difficulty maintaining public trust in our professions today.

For years colleges and universities have offered remedial courses in the basic skills for students deficient in those areas. Perhaps we should consider a remedial course in ethics. Maybe we ought to disperse philosophers and religious studies scholars into our professional schools (a practice already in place in selected universities).

The impulse to goodness springs not from government nor corporate structures, not from committees and councils. The impulse to goodness begins in units of one, in the heart and mind of each professional. Whatever combination of approaches we may use to achieve it, renewing ethical force in our professions is essential.

The Making of a Servant Professional

While many are asking how teaching can become more of a profession like medicine and law, I would go further and ask how to make teaching a *servant* profession. John Gardner (1986), one of our nation's most perceptive writers on the nature of leadership, has this to say about the professions:

> The professions dominate much of contemporary life, and they are not noted for their belief in the idea of leadership. As one listens to some of the ablest people in graduate and professional education, one gets the impression that they are saying, in effect, "Let us train an elite class of gifted professionals and let them cope with the future as experts, not leaders: bright, orderly minded, analytically gifted experts who will identify the problems, gather the relevant data, test possible solutions and proceed to the goal." But most professionals become specialists, and they have a powerful impulse to deal with only those aspects of a problem that fit their specialty. Leaders are generalists. An additional handicap of professionals is that they have generally had no occasion to develop the political sensitivity that leadership requires — may indeed have been schooled to be contemptuous of things political. (p. 16)

In my view, the concept of the servant profession can overcome the problems outlined by Gardner: a narrowness of interest and perspective, a contempt for political concerns. And the concept of the servant profession is a bulwark against professional confidence becoming professional arrogance, which in my mind is the most dangerous of professional liabilities.

The servant profession is marked by:

Nobility of purpose — service to improvement of society and humankind.

71

Systematic knowledge foundation — a body of ideas and concepts to guide decision making.

Rigorous selection and education — a process attending to the intellectual, clinical, and ethical development of persons.

Governance of competence — the authority and means to deal with standards of practice and questions of incompetent professional behavior.

Linkage to laity — the active involvement of laypersons on policy issues related to professional preparation, licensure, and practice, including cost effectiveness and effectiveness of practice.

I already have commented on the above qualities of the servant profession. This entire book is devoted to the nobility of purpose in teaching. In Chapter Five I dealt with both the legacy and the limitations of the knowledge foundation in education. And in this chapter I have argued that teaching is actively linked to the laity. Yes, it is from the laity that some of the strongest criticism of the schools has come; but it is also laity who give recognition to the achievements of our schools. On this point, we might well attend to comments from former Tennessee governor Lamar Alexander, writing in the *Kettering Review* (Fall 1985):

> Maybe it's just human nature to worry that an attack on our schools is an attack on those who work in the system. Whatever the reason, there is nothing fair about blaming teachers for whatever ails our public schools.
>
> Why not honor teachers again? If we do not, the better schools movement — which depends upon excellence in teaching — will in the long run fail. And especially while we are in the midst of reform, our reform message needs to be clear and unequivocal:
>
> We respect your caring, your patience and your competence. We are grateful to you. The better schools movement is a salute to your importance. We are going to do our best to reward your excellence, improve your working conditions, create opportunities for you to sense more of your accomplishment — and, most importantly — find more ways to confer honor and respect upon what you do. (pp. 44-45)

Who are these teachers we need to honor? Here is one servant professional. JoAmi Wynn teaches mathematics at Captain Shreve High School in Shreveport, a comprehensive high school cited earlier. Her day starts as early as 5:00 a.m. with work on her lesson plans for the day — a few precious moments captured before her family arises. She arrives at school around 7:00 a.m. and spends 30 to 40 minutes coaching individual students in need of special help. Every day she teaches five one-hour periods and has one hour for planning, running off tests, and grading papers.

At 2:15 in the afternoon she spends another hour or more giving individual help to students. She gives other time to coaching the school's quiz bowl team and sponsoring the National Honor Society. On most nights she spends from two to three hours grading and correcting papers for approximately 125 students she teaches each day. She's been doing this for almost 25 years.

JoAmi is devoted to young people and dedicated to excellence in teaching. Each day she stands at her classroom door and greets each student with a smile and personal comment, affirming in that small but important act the worth and dignity of all entrusted to her care. She is living testimony of what Emerson describes as "Every great and commanding moment is the triumph of some enthusiasm." Here is a servant professional who manifests an enthusiasm in each of her classes. "Teaching was what I was meant to do!" is the simple way she expresses her professionalism.

Cynics may deny the evidence of JoAmi's goodness. But not her students. On several occasions she has been nominated as outstanding teacher in the parish, and she has been named Outstanding PTA Teacher in Louisiana. JoAmi is not a writer. She is not a researcher. She is a teacher. She lives, loves, and labors in a high school, where her reality is the importance of the Pythagorean and binomial theorems in developing the potential of the lives entrusted to her care.

Now the cynics may also argue that JoAmi Wynn is an aberration, a case study not truly representative of teachers. They have a vision of dull and plodding folks neither competent nor caring. They have a vision of strident teacher union leaders more interested in increasing teacher salaries than in the needs of pupils. They have a vision of timid educators unwilling to discipline their own ranks. I do not doubt the existence of these unfortunate models in the profession. What I do doubt is that the prevalence or percentage of the arrogant or ignorant professional in teaching is any greater than in any other profession.

One builds a servant profession by honoring the best models. JoAmi Wynn is one of those models. She represents an ideal of teaching that is valid in both my experience and my research. Her life is gentle but passionate. Her voice is sweet but confident. Her spirit is trusting but discerning. Her teaching is a study in quiet nobility. She is a servant professional.

References

Alexander, Lamar. "Honor Thy Teachers." *Kettering Review* (Fall 1985).

Carnegie Task Force on Teaching as a Profession. *A Nation Prepared: Teachers for the 21st Century*. New York: Carnegie Forum on Education and the Economy, May 1986.

Eble, Kenneth W. *The Craft of Teaching*. San Francisco: Jossey-Bass, 1976.

Gardner, John W. *Leadership and Power. Leadership Papers 4*. Washington, D.C.: Leadership Studies Program Independent Sector, October 1986.

Gilbert, Highet. *The Immortal Profession*. New York: Weybright and Talley, 1976.

Goodlad, John I.; Soder, Roger; and Sirotnik, Kenneth A., eds. *The Moral Dimensions of Teaching*. San Francisco: Jossey-Bass, 1990.

Green, Joslyn, ed. *What Next? More Leverage for Teachers*. Denver: Education Commission of the States, July 1986.

The Holmes Group. *Tomorrow's Teachers*. East Lansing, Mich., April 1986.

King, John E. "Should We Abolish the Bachelor's Degree in Education: Absolutely Not." *Change Magazine* (September/October 1986).

Lewis, Anne C. "Washington Commentary: Different Strokes?" *Phi Delta Kappan* (January 1990).

Lieberman, Myron. "A Botched Attempt at Education Reform." *World and I Magazine* (September 1986).

National Governors' Association. *Time for Results: The Governors' 1991 Report on Education*. Washington, D.C., August 1986.

Southern Regional Education Board. "Major Reports on Teacher Education: What Do They Mean for States?" *Regional Spotlight* (October 1986).

Shanker, Albert. *The Making of a Profession*. Edited transcript of remarks of Albert Shanker before the Representative Assembly of the New York State United Teachers in Niagara Falls, 27 April 1985.

Smith, B. Othanel. *A Design for a School of Pedagogy*. Washington, D.C.: U.S. Department of Education, 1980.

Woodring, Paul. "School Teaching Cannot be Considered a Profession as Long as Its Entrance Standards Remain so Low." *Chronicle of Higher Education*, 23 November 1986.

SEVEN
A Real World

Bow down thine ear, and hear the words of the wise,
and apply thine heart unto my knowledge.

Proverbs 22:17

A few years ago I was invited to be the commencement speaker at LeTourneau College in Longview, Texas. Named after R.G. LeTourneau, an American inventor genius who never finished the seventh grade, this little college for years has been sending graduates all over the world, many into Christian mission fields. Yet it may be less well known in the region where I live than it is in some of the cities and countries from which students come and return.

The college's programs center primarily on engineering and engineering technology. All programs are accredited by the Accrediting Board for Engineering and Technology, the national engineering accrediting agency — a quality recognition of no small achievement for any engineering college and certainly for one of this size. The quiet work going on at LeTourneau College and the achievements of its students rarely make headlines. Whether it has ever been on any of the "best lists" of colleges that appear in national magazines from time to time, I do not know. Yet the story of this college illustrates the rich diversity of the American higher education system.

Here is an educational climate different from Harvard, Cal Tech, or Oberlin. Here is an educational world different from my own university just 60 miles away. LeTourneau struggles to maintain its financial health and to establish a proper balance between its technical programs and humanities, while at the same time interpreting its Christian mission. It is one of the small jewels of American higher education. Its brilliance may not be noticed among the larger and more visible institutions. But here among the rolling hills of East Texas is an educational institution whose power to influence the world may be more potent than that of much larger and more prestigious institutions.

As I wait to be introduced as the commencement speaker, I wonder what thoughts circulate in the minds of those graduating and of their parents, spouses, and friends. No doubt some hearts are filled with pride for the achievement represented in the degree earned; some hearts are filled with excitement and anxiety as they anticipate their next steps upon exiting the portals of LeTourneau into the so-called real world. Leaving behind this educational sanctuary of soccer fields and aviation laboratories, some will be flying missionaries into remote jungles a short time hence, while others will be untangling the mysteries of a computer payroll program in a small company in St. Paul, Minnesota. Are they graduating to the real world or just a different world?

The conventional view is that the "real world" awaits outside the doors of schools and colleges. This view implies that those who teach are shielded from the harsher realities of life, that schools and colleges are places of ideals and ideas, currencies of low practical value out there in the real world. It implies that schools and colleges are places of preparation and perhaps not worth savoring for their own value. It implies that those who labor in schools and colleges are buffered from pressures of competition and "bottom line" mentality of that real world beyond diplomas and degrees.

I understand this often-voiced distinction, but I do not agree with it. It is difficult for me to accept that my quarter-century as an educator has been a journey of lesser reality than for those who have been working for Prudential, AT&T, or First National Bank. It is, to be sure, a different reality — perhaps a more important and even dangerous reality.

In my view, the faculty in our schools and colleges are deeply involved in defining reality. Our history courses and textbooks tell us what is important to remember about the past realities, even defining that past reality through the mind and pen of the historian. What we teach in literature, music, and drama reveals the reality of humanity's aspirations and achievements, its failures and frustrations. Our courses in philosophy, ethics, and theology plumb the realities of our values. In science and mathematics we find the instruments for the discovery and creation of new realities. The practical man may march to the power of a single idea — an idea born in a study, a classroom, or a laboratory. Schools and colleges are most intimately

76

involved in defining what is real, preserving what is real, and creating what is real.

Schools and colleges are also places where students begin to have their first awareness of life's three most basic questions: For what purpose will I invest my life? What means and methods will I choose to realize that purpose? And how will I measure success in life? Here's a poetic engagement of those questions by James Kavanaugh:

Somewhere Along the Way*

Somewhere along the way
A persistent voice taught me I was in competition
With every other man in the world.
I listened carefully
And learned the lesson well.
It was not enough
To find a loving wife and have average, happy kids,
To see a sunrise and wonder at an eclipsing moon,
To enjoy a meal and catch a trout in a silent, silver river,
To picnic in a meadow at the top of a mountain
Or ride horses along the rim of a hidden lake,
To laugh like a child at midnight
And to still wonder about the falling stars.
It was only enough
To be admired and powerful and to rush from one success to
    another,
To barely see faces or hear voices, to ignore beauty and forget
    music,
To reduce everything and everybody to a stereo color
pattern on the way to some new triumph.
To rest in no victory, but to create new and more demanding
goals even as I seem to succeed,
Until finally I was estranged and exhausted, victorious and
joyless, successful and ready to abandon life.
Then somewhere along the way
I remembered the laugh of a child I once knew,
I saw a familiar boy wandering joyously in the woods,
I felt a heart pounding with excitement at the birth of a new day,
Until I was in competition with no one and life was clear again,
Somewhere along the way.

---

*Copyright by James Kavanaugh. Reprinted by permission.

Are students not living in the real world as they engage these questions in schools and colleges?

I recently had the occasion to address a leadership seminar of some 200 young high school sophomores. In the question-and-answer session following my remarks, one of the young students nailed me to the wall with this question: "Is it okay to aspire to be valedictorian of your class, to have that achievement as a goal?" His question engages the three elements of goals, means, and success. This was my response:

"Perhaps that would be a worthy goal. But answering that question also involves a question of means, a question of success. Suppose that you and I both wanted to be valedictorian. Suppose that you and I were in a dead heat on grade point average going into our final year. And suppose that I was going to take calculus in my final year, a subject of some complexity and intellectual risk. And suppose that you decided that if you took an easier course, say typewriting, then you might stand a better chance of beating my GPA and thus becoming valedictorian. That's an interesting interaction among goal, means, and success."

I then went on to say, "Perhaps you should worry less about becoming valedictorian than in giving your best effort to those courses and experiences that would serve you well in the future. If you happened to become valedictorian, then that might be a pleasant and happy byproduct of more important ends and means."

From this group of 200 bright sophomores, some would be selected for further leadership roles, including the opportunity to attend a national leadership seminar. They were all being evaluated by the seminar counselors in attendance as well as by their student colleagues. You could see them struggling with questions of self and society that you can find in any corporate board room or business office.

A few had put on false personalities, a facade of another self. A few had succumbed to a narrow stereotype of what they thought leadership should look like and behave like — young versions of The Man in the Grey Flannel Suit or The Corporate Woman. A few were overwhelmed and decided they didn't stand a chance and removed themselves from the competition. And a few decided to be themselves and let the evaluation chips fall where they may. All 200 were learning lessons that were very real to them. More important, they were learning habits and values they would apply in similar settings throughout their lives. In this weekend leadership seminar, they were beginning to learn about multiple realities of life.

Multiple Realities of Schooling

Schools and colleges are the places where we begin to learn about and experience multiple realities. Foremost, they are places where we learn how to access reality. Schools and colleges have a pre-eminent role in advancing truth and constructing reality.

Students learn to use the intellectual tools in the various fields of study to analyze, to synthesize, and to make judgments. They also learn how a tool such as mathematics can be used across disciplines to show relationships. Indeed, mathematics is the major tool we have for communicating scientific truth. In the real world of school and college, then, we begin to discover reality.

But human beings do more than simply discern reality. They hold in their hands the power to create. They are the architects of new realities — creating wheels and axles, clocks and levers, steamboats and airplanes, lasers and computers, geometries and calculus. One need only look back on this century to see human creativity at work: major advances in transportation via airplanes and rockets, the unleashing of nuclear energy, the advent of the computer, the harnessing of electricity for powerful new communication systems, and unlocking the genetic code enabling us to eradicate certain diseases.

In our schools and colleges we create models of reality and then we make them obsolete. In the 1950s when I studied physics in college, the dominant model used to explain the structure of the atom was the Bohr model, using a planetary analogy. There was the nucleus, composed of neutrons and protons. Swirling about the nucleus like small planets were the electrons, each occupying, according to Bohr's theory, discrete energy levels. When the electrons changed energy levels, one could predict the color of light emitted. Indeed, each element had its own distinctive spectrographic pattern. The theory was very satisfying, very elegant. The only trouble is, it may have been all wrong, just as the Ptolemaic conception of the universe was all wrong — even though the mathematical calculations and predictions derived from the theory were good approximations. We can create models of reality that seem to have great practical utility, only to find over time that the models we have created are imperfect or erroneous.

In addition to discovering and creating physical realities, we create other realities as well through our values and expectations. The research reported in *Pygmalion in the Classroom* (Rosenthal and Jacobson 1968) and "Pygmalion in Management" (Livingston 1969) documents a basic element of human behavior; namely, that the expectations we hold for the behavior of others is a key determinant in what kind of behavior we elicit. We are more likely to elicit trust and independence, for example, if we expect trust and independence. If we expect high performance from students, we are more likely get to high performance.

Over the past few years I have taught a graduate seminar on the topic of leadership. The basic theme of the seminar is that leadership is an art form composed of both technical and ethical elements. I make the point that some leaders jeopardize their organizations not because of their lack of technical competence but because they prostitute their integrity — an ethical issue.

I introduce the seminar with a series of questions on leadership that cover both technical and ethical issues. Here are some of the issues I cover:

1. Role — Visionary vs. Facilitator: What is the role of the leader? Does he or she set direction or ask others to find direction?
2. Motivation — Fear vs. Love: What are the major motives for human behavior? Do we act from fear or love? Or both? What are the motivating elements of competition and cooperation?
3. Effectiveness — Process vs. Outcome: How do we evaluate the effectiveness of leader behavior? Of organizations? How is morale related to organizational and personal achievement?
4. Efficiency — Technology vs. Personnel: What responsibility does the leader have to make efficient use of human and technical resources? What are the keys to improved productivity? How does productivity differ from quality and efficiency?
5. Decision — Reflection vs. Action: How does the leader's decision-making style relate to decision type and decision climate? What are the legitimate sources of leader authority and how are these most effectively applied?
6. Change — Risk vs. Security: How does the leader orchestrate change in an organization?
7. Organization — Ambiguity vs. Structure: What kinds of organizational structures are available to the leader? When can structure be facilitating and when impeding? Is bureaucracy all bad?
8. Conflict — Order vs. Justice: What role do dissent and disorder play in leader and organizational health?
9. Leadership Style — Task Orientation vs. Personal Orientation: How can the leader identify his or her dominant style? Is there

an effective style? What do we know of the relationship between leader personality and organizational function?

In schools and colleges, then, we begin to learn about the reality of values: arrogance vs. humility, jealousy vs. self-reliance, prejudice vs. compassion, cowardice vs. courage. What student has not seen the incubation of these values in his or her life, whether in the classroom and laboratory or on the playing field?

Here is a young reporter for an award-winning college newspaper. She is attractive and talented, destined for a promising career in journalism. Perhaps within that talent is the potential for a Pulitzer Prize. But while in college she is about to learn important lessons, not only about writing but about living. She has a lead on an important story involving local politics, a chance to scoop the major metropolitan dailies in her city. But to get the story might require the use of her sexual charm to loosen the tongue of a certain party for the information she needs. Does the end justify the means? In the answer she chooses, she will have begun the creation of her own reality.

Yes, the world of school and college is a real world. The values beginning to take shape there will create, in part, the kind of real world in which students will live after school. In this sense, then, school is a more critical and dangerous real world. It is also an exciting and satisfying real world, which is why teachers like it there.

The Meaning of Reality

This morning, after goodbye hugs for my wife and three children, I am smiling as I leave for work at 7:15 a.m. with briefcase in hand. Within an hour, however, my smile will yield to tears. I have been invited to a breakfast at Holy Angels Center. The center, operated by the Catholic Church, is a living-and-learning facility for children with various degrees of mental retardation and physical handicaps. The school is operated as an attendance center by the Caddo Parish public school system. This breakfast is a venture to make the public more aware of the challenges and achievements in our public schools. I have attended several of these breakfasts — at Pine Grove Elementary, Caddo Middle Magnet, Captain Shreve High School — but this is my first visit to Holy Angels.

It is a pleasant morning as I drive along tree-shaded Ellerbe Road. The rays of early morning sun filter through the leaves and paint soft patterns in the air. Across from the well-kept and attractive grounds of Holy Angels is an affluent, new residential development, one of many marking this area as one of the more attractive places to live in Shreveport.

After breakfast, we go to visit the children. Here is four-year-old Mark, whose cerebral palsy is so severe he cannot even roll over. His teacher works not on the usual tasks of the early childhood classroom but simply on trying to get Mark to raise and turn his head. I turn to five-year-old Cathy with big blue eyes and blonde hair that falls loosely around her contorted face. What do those big blue eyes see? She is strapped to a board in upright position as her teacher tries to teach her the simple task of chewing her food. Tears emerge unbidden and roll down my face as I wonder at the gift of my three healthy children back home — and at the devotion and patience of these teachers.

In front of Holy Angels Center out on Ellerbe Road, folks move past in their Hondas and Oldsmobiles, listening to morning news and music on their car radios as they head for work to engage a production problem at AT&T, a new account challenge at Peat, Marwick, and Mitchell, a new land lease for Crystal Oil Company, an investment venture at Commercial National Bank, a new warehouse project at Trammell Crow, an engineering problem at the Pennzoil Refinery. But little Cathy and her teacher know nothing of these realities on this sunny morning. It will be a wonderful day if only Cathy will chew the bite of scrambled eggs her teacher has placed in her mouth. Theirs is a different reality.

Yes, in our schools and colleges we engage multiple realities. We discern and discover truth through science and history. We express truth through drama, music, literature, and art. We test the truth through experiment and argument. We also create reality by constructing models of the physical world that enable us to predict and control. Sometimes our models and our theories become obsolete and lead to newer models with new realities. And the values we develop in school and college are important in creating social, political, and economic realities. But there may yet be a larger, more embracing question of reality. It is the search for what gives meaning to our lives, a search that constitutes one of the major motives for human existence. Schools and colleges are instruments of this search.

Ed Hearon, principal at Broadmoor Middle School in Shreveport, is one of those educators dedicated to finding and giving meaning to his faculty, his students, and his community. When you visit Ed's school, you always find him smiling and enthusiastic. He wears the distinctive maroon blazer that he and his staff have adopted to build pride in the school. Most of Ed's teachers have a master's degree, and many work with student teachers. All teach under an open-door policy, with their classrooms open for observation at any time of day by parents or other visitors.

When Ed assumed the principalship at Broadmoor, the school's enrollment was about 300. This past year, enrollment was approximately 800; and parents camped in front of the school all night to secure a place for their children in this alternative public school. Students contract to enter Ed's school. They must maintain a 90% attendance record and a satisfactory conduct record.

But Ed and his faculty know about other kinds of reality. This past year, he and his faculty were saddened by the suicide death of a popular, 13-year-old honor student who had been active in school activities. Somewhere along the way, she lost sight of the future, lost her hold on life's meaning. She was very neat about it. Left her parents a note, told them not to blame themselves, and took her life with a revolver in the bathroom so as not to mess up the house. A shock for Ed, his faculty, his students. But this is not Ed's first encounter with difficult moments of life.

He and his wife have three boys. The first two were healthy boys, fine young men who now play basketball like their dad. But the third little fellow was born with Down's Syndrome. And so Ed knows what it's like to hurt as both parent and educator. Because he knows that struggle and suffering bring meaning to life as well, he is a stronger and more sensitive educator.

In the real world of schooling, then, we engage our students with multiple realities. We teach them to discern and create reality. We help them find meaning in struggle, service, and suffering as well as in achievement, joy, and pleasure. We help them fashion a vision of their future. We encourage them to ask each day what there has been to make them glad to be alive. We enable them to construct a real world. We rejoice for those who construct a world of giving rather than taking, who find meaning and nobility of purpose in their lives. And we search our hearts and hurt for those who waste their talent and potential in living suicide.

References

Kavanaugh, James. *Maybe If I Loved You More*. Highland Park, Ill.: Steven J. Nash, 1990.

Livingston, J. Sterling. "Pygmalion in Management." *Harvard Business Review* (July-August 1969).

Rosenthal, Robert, and Jacobson, Lenore. *Pygmalion in the Classroom*. New York: Holt, Rinehart, and Winston, 1968.

EIGHT
A Journey of the Heart

Happy is the man that findeth wisdom,
and the man that getteth understanding.
For the merchandise of it is better than
the merchandise of silver, and the gain
thereof than fine gold.

Proverbs 3:13-14

Over in Bronson Hall on the Louisiana State University-Shreveport campus, three of our master teachers are at work. As chancellor I often hear compliments on the artistry of Donald Smith, who teaches mathematics and computer science. Stock brokers, attorneys, retired AT&T executives, teachers, and bright-faced 18-year-olds all sing the praises of his teaching talent.

Just two doors down, Karen Douglas is teaching literature. In addition to her teaching, Karen writes specialty pieces for our local papers. She also writes poetry, which has been published in such journals as *Atlantic Monthly*. To read or listen to Karen's poetry is to know you are in the presence of a precious talent. With an economy of words, she creates whole mountains of thought and feelings of wonder and awe. Karen's poetry unfolds in a university setting whose existence is possible only because the profit and service sectors of our society exist in symbiotic relationship.

On the third floor, John Hall regales an audience of students and faculty colleagues with a non-credit lecture on "The Social History of Whiskey." He and his wife, Carol, who also teaches at the university, conduct European tours sponsored by the university. Last year John taught a geography course on the tour, making learning come alive as his students experienced geography firsthand. John also was among the prime movers in bringing to our campus and community a "Pioneer Heritage" museum reflecting the cultural heritage of northern Louisiana, which is very different from the Cajun heritage most often associated with the state. I receive compliments from a variety of people in the community, oil company executives, prominent jurists, nurses who have attended John's lectures and interesting travelogues.

Donald and John have been teaching for more than 20 years, Karen a little more than 10. Their salaries do not begin to match the salaries of some of those they teach (physicians, attorneys, stockbrokers) nor the future salaries of their promising younger students. In recent years they have not had a raise because of the poor economic conditions in Louisiana. Why do they come to the classroom every day? I can see it in their faces, in their smiles reflecting the satisfaction of seeing young minds open to new understanding, in their responses to compliments received for their artistry and talent, in the satisfaction derived from their own creativity. Their teaching is of a quality that emerges only when a genuine talent is joyously united in doing good work.

In *The Immortal Profession*, Gilbert Highet (1976) closes his introductory chapter on "The Pleasures of Learning" with this note: "The chief aim of education is to show you, *after* you make a living, how to enjoy living; and you can live longest and best and most rewardingly by attaining and preserving the happiness of learning" (p. 19). Imagine the fun in work devoted to both provoking and preserving the "happiness of learning."

Donald, John, and Karen find pleasure in their work, as do hundred of elementary and secondary school colleagues in Shreveport. Take Carol Cathey. She teaches second grade at Arthur Circle School, an elementary school serving a modest but neat neighborhood in Shreveport. She has been teaching for several years. Her experiences range from having her class give her a surprise baby shower to receiving threats from a 200-pound bullying parent. She sums up her convictions on teaching with this comment: "Teaching is the hardest job in the world if you do it right and the easiest if you don't care!"

Donald, John, Karen, Carol — why would these fine teachers and the thousands of others who serve in our classrooms each day continue in a profession that is so frequently subjected to public criticism? Why would they continue in a profession that is among the lowest paid in our society? Why would they continue in a profession that often commands little respect and often seems to be the least valued?

Perhaps it's because they can't do anything else. They are called to teaching.

A Call to Teaching

Cynics delight in saying that those who teach do so only because their frail spirits and weak minds couldn't handle the hard realities in life, and so they retreat to the warm and protected womb of the classroom. Leaving aside the ignorance and insensitivity of those who have never known the emotional and physical drains that come from working in those classrooms, the labors of love and defeat that I have described throughout these essays, I believe that many, perhaps most, teachers teach because they are called.

We are familiar with the religious connotation of the word "call." As ministers are called to their work, I believe that the best among our teachers are called to their work. Whether God whispered in their ear I cannot say, but they would not want to do anything else with their lives. They are teachers because heart, mind, and soul sing to their work, because they know the joy of touching lives and influencing the future for good.

Although my primary duties as chancellor of a university are administrative, I try to teach at least one class each year and encourage my administrative colleagues to do likewise, so that we all remember why we are there. In a graduate seminar I taught recently, I had the pleasure of working with students from a variety of backgrounds: a TV reporter, a museum curator, an attorney, a chamber of commerce executive, a teacher, a public-relations executive, a Junior League officer, a city planner. One evening, one of the students brought me a little plaque on which was written these words: "To Teach is to Touch a Life Forever." I treasure that gift. I treasure more the eternal truth of the message.

Teaching is a journey of the heart! I can still remember the first teacher that started me on my journey. Mrs. Oma Oglesby was my first-grade teacher at Millington Elementary School in Millington, Tennessee. Several years earlier, she had taught my older brother, "Bubba." When my dad died while I was still a boy, Bubba became both brother and father to me. It was his car that I borrowed for my first dates in high school. It was his life of hard work, family devotion, and personal integrity that served as a model for me. When I entered the first grade in 1941, Bubba was beginning his four years in the Army Engineer Corps in the Pacific. Bubba returned from the war and began work as a yard superintendent for a concrete-products company in Memphis. Mrs. Oglesby must have given him a good start, because he retired recently, having served as president of that company for more than 15 years.

Who knows what promise resides in the young children awaiting the touch of the artist teacher? As my first-grade class sat in a circle around Mrs. Oglesby in 1941 singing "The Farmer in the Dell," what could she have known about the potential in chubby faced "Sonny" Bogue, other than that I was the little brother of "Bubba" Bogue, whom she had taught years earlier. Indeed, what could I have known about myself? That Bubba Bogue would advance to a leadership position in the business world, that Sonny Bogue would go on to become a university chancellor — I doubt that Mrs. Oglesby could have discerned that potential in either Bubba or me. But she was called to a precious work, and we were fortunate to benefit from her caring touch.

Teachers teach because they can't do anything else! Why? Because they have a love for learning. I can still remember moments of discovery in Mrs. Miller's second-grade class back in 1942 in Millington Elementary School. We were learning to count, first to a hundred and then to a thousand. I remember the excitement I felt once I learned the pattern of tens and how I could take the pattern and construct numbers as far as my imagination could take me. And I remember the knowing smile when I ran with my lined tablet to show Mrs. Miller what I had discovered.

My mind as a second-grader could not conceptualize something called "imaginary" numbers reflected in the square root of minus 1. This was yet another new and exciting concept I derived from the teaching of my high school algebra teacher, Kathleen Tenant, and my college physics professor, Carrol Ijams. In my own excitement of discovery, I failed to see their pleasure as my understanding moved outward to new horizons.

In graduate school I studied the statistical concept of analysis of variance, one of the fundamental tools of inferential statistics used in both physical and social science. I learned to calculate the analysis of variance, first on my hand-held calculator and then later using the computer. I conducted research studies and I wrote reports using this important conceptual tool, but I did not really understand the theoretical underpinning for analysis of variance until I began teaching a course in research design.

One day as I was working on my lesson plan, I remember breaking into a big grin and exclaiming, "I got it!" Two colleagues who shared the same office gave me a puzzled look. What they didn't know was that while I understood the outward contours of the analysis of variance, it was not until I began teaching the concept to others that I could conceptualize how the tool had been constructed and why it worked. Yet there are many things I could not teach. I have a general understanding of how the internal combustion engine works in my Chevrolet Suburban. But the instructor over at the Caddo Parish Career Center who teaches his students to take that engine apart and put it back together again imparts to them a level of understanding about internal combustion, which I don't understand, much less could ever teach.

Will Durant opens his monumental *The Story of Civilization* (1954) with these words:

> Civilization is social order promoting cultural creation. Four elements constitute it: economic provision, political organization, moral traditions, and the pursuit of knowledge and the arts. It begins where chaos and insecurity end. For when fear is overcome, curiosity and constructiveness are free, and may pass by natural impulse toward the understanding and embellishment of life.

In the "pursuit of knowledge and the arts," teachers and their students find a delightful menu of learning to stimulate their curiosity. Teachers find pleasure not only in seeing the lights turn on in the minds of their students but also in probing the deeper meaning of the subject they are teaching.

Teachers teach because they can't do anything else. Why? Because they have a love for learners. Talk to a group of teachers about their motivations for choosing teaching as a career and you likely will find that they say they have a love for children. This love of learners is no small matter. I have met any number of bright folks who are preparing to become teachers. They can pass the courses in both their teaching field and pedagogy with ease. The problem comes when they get to the clinical part of their preparation, student teaching. Some of them discover at this point that they simply don't like being around learners. We could say that it is sad to find at the end of your college preparation that you have misdirected your energies. But we might also give thanks that we did not receive into our classrooms a teacher without a love for learners.

Mrs. Parker was my son Barrett's first-grade teacher. What pleasure she must have derived in watching her 25 little charges finish the year with skills they didn't start with. She had visible evidence of the children's progress as they began reading books on their own, writing simple sentences for stories they composed, and using mathematical concepts including some elements of algebra. She can take great satisfaction in having guided the children in developing the readiness that will take them to the next step on the learning ladder.

Her heart will hurt, though, because some of her little ones will not find in their home or family life the support needed to develop their potential. The hurt will be frustrating because she will be powerless in some instances to overcome the negative forces in their lives. And she will wonder at some who seem to overcome every adversity, those strong little personalities who have found some spark — perhaps because Mrs. Parker has lifted their vision or touched their lives in some special way that helped them overcome the barriers of neglect and deprivation.

There is neither history nor biography to reveal the evidence of Mrs. Parker's love for learners at Stoner Hill Elementary School in Shreveport, Louisiana. That evidence will be found in the lives she touched. Years later, some will look back in gratitude with the same fondness I have for my first-grade teacher, Mrs. Oma Oglesby, who invested her caring in my life. Her caring and that of other teachers in my life I now honor by investing that caring in the lives of those I teach. And I can draw the same pleasure in watching their talents unfold.

How can I measure the value of the lessons I learned from my students: a respect for the great diversity of their personalities, a wonder at how high expectations led them to high achievement, an appreciation of their compelling questions and maverick spirits, an expansion of my mental and emotional capacities brought by their challenges and their performances? Teaching is a journey of the heart.

Teachers teach because they can't do anything else. Why? Because they have a gift to give. Here is a letter inviting me to come and read to Cindy Dolch's third-grade class at Waller Elementary School in Bossier City, just across the river from Shreveport. Cindy is the wife of Norman Dolch, one of our fine professors in the Sociology Department. Apparently, Cindy has invited a number of civic figures to come and read to her children during the year.

This is a renewing opportunity in the life of a college chancellor. I put aside policy ventures with the Faculty Senate, uncertain conditions in the state legislature, the press to raise private money for the university, and have my secretary schedule the time. Now what to read? I have been probing the mysteries of new mathematics in James Gleick's *Chaos* (1987), the marvels of multiple intelligences in Robert Sternberg's *The Triarchic Mind* (1988), and the fruits of our aloneness in Anthony Storr's *Solitude* (1988). These books, I conclude, are not going to cut it with third-graders.

Thinking about what to read to these third-graders affirms a feeling I've had for a long time and have expressed in these essays — that the most inspired and imaginative teaching is likely to take place in our kindergartens and elementary schools. Those busy little minds and bodies will not willingly tolerate dull lectures and pedantic plodding, as will some college and adult students. In Cindy Dolch's third-grade classroom, you teach or you get a room full of customer dissatisfaction. So I go home and scan the books I treasure that sit on shelves above my desk. Then I wander into my daughter's room and look over her little library. Now here are some good possibilities that will allow me to survive for 30 or 40 minutes in Cindy's classroom. I pick out the classic *The Little Engine That Could* (1984) and Shel Silverstein's delightful book of poetry *Where the Sidewalk Ends* (1974).

The children are reasonably attentive to the little engine story, as I try to make the point that we need to believe in ourselves. One or two assertive little folks on the front row interact with me. And a couple of shy ones in the back have their eyes hidden on the floor. But they all warm up to the poem "Captain Hook," which evokes many giggles.

Captain Hook*

Captain Hook must remember
Not to scratch his toes.
Captain Hook must watch out
And never pick his nose.
Captain Hook must be gentle
When he shakes your hand.
Captain Hook must be careful
Openin' sardine cans
And playing tag and pouring tea
And turnin' pages of his book.
Lots of Folks I'm glad I ain't —
But Mostly Captain Hook!

---

*Copyright by Shel Silverstein. Reprinted by permission.

The afternoon ends with a lot of laugher. The children seemed to have enjoyed my reading. I leave Waller Elementary School with a renewed spirit and a fresh appreciation for the thousands of teachers like Cindy Dolch who spend each day giving the gift of love — praising and prodding, confronting and comforting, arguing and affirming.

In *The Prophet* (1969, p. 56) Gibran speaks of teaching in this way: "The teacher who walks in the shadow of the temple, among his followers, gives not of his wisdom but rather of his faith and lovingness." Faith and lovingness. These are great and mysterious gifts. These are the gifts that once given come back to the giver with greater value and beauty. Teachers have a gift to give. This is why teachers teach. This is why teachers take a journey of the heart.

References

Durant, Will. *Our Oriental Heritage: The Story of Civilization, Part I.* New York: Simon and Schuster, 1954.

Gibran, Kahlil. *The Prophet.* New York: Knopf, 1969.

Gleick, James. *Chaos: Making a New Science.* New York: Viking, 1987.

Highet, Gilbert. *The Immortal Profession.* New York: Weybright and Talley, 1976.

Piper, Watty. *The Little Engine That Could.* New York: Platt and Munk, 1984.

Silverstein, Shel. *Where the Sidewalk Ends.* New York: Harper & Row, 1974.

Sternberg, Robert J. *The Triarchic Mind: A New Theory of Human Intelligence.* New York: Viking, 1988.

Storr, Anthony. *Solitude: A Return to the Self.* New York: Free Press, 1988.

NINE
A Promise to Keep

How have I hated instruction, and my heart despised reproof;
And have not obeyed the voice of my teachers,
not inclined my heart to them that instructed me.

Proverbs 5:12-13

I played hooky this morning — at least from the university. To-day my youngest child, Michael, is taking a field trip with his Stoner Hill Elementary School kindergarten class to the Central Fire Station and then on to Betty Virginia Park for a few moments of play. Early this morning, he wanted to know if his mother and I might make the field trip with him.

Why not? We need to cultivate special moments of interruption in our scheduled lives. Commencement last evening ended the spring term and the academic year at the university. A quick phone call to the office revealed only one appointment, which could be re-arranged. Off with the tie and on with the sport shirt. Away for a morning with the children.

The children filed off the yellow school bus in orderly fashion, holding hands with teachers and assorted chaperones, including the university chancellor. We entered the cavernous interior of the Central Fire Station, where one of Shreveport's finest began his presentation on the equipment used on one of the large white pumper units. Next came one of the most fun activities, donning the fireman's helmet, heavy fire coat, and large rubber boots. But this fun was abruptly interrupted when the station's alarm went off. Heretofore unseen firemen came sliding down the four brass poles, and the big white pumper went roaring out of the station with bells clanging and sirens wailing.

In all the tumult, Michael grabbed his mother's hand tightly, while his buddy, Terry, leaped into my arms, where he remained throughout the rest of the tour. When the excitement died down, we continued our tour to the ladder and emergency service units, then up the stairs to the sleeping quarters, recreation room, kitchen, and classroom facilities. I finally coaxed Terry to take his fingers out of his ears when we got to peek through the red doors behind which were the brass poles the firemen had descended only moments before.

Michael's kindergarten teacher, Miss Vassar, told me later that Terry came from a home where there was very limited exposure to outside activities. These school outings, she explained, are enriching for Terry, even though he is extremely cautious about anything that is new and different. He needed to be hugged at this moment, and I felt a bit of trust building between him and me. We were pretty good friends by the time we hit the playground at Betty Virginia Park, but he was still casting suspicious eyes about for lurking fire engines and their wailing sirens.

At Stoner Hill Elementary School, 25 little kindergartners arrive every day, each from a different home climate, each presenting a different challenge for Miss Vassar. In Shreveport we build trucks, transformers, and telephones in three major manufacturing facilities. The raw materials used in these products are tested at entry and at each step along the assembly line to ensure a quality product at exit. Miss Vassar, however, has no quality control over what these little children bring to her classroom each day.

A special issue of *Newsweek* (Winter/Spring 1990) is devoted to "The 21st Century Family." It reports many things that we already know about what's happening to our families, but the statistics alone do not give us insight into the tragedy of too many American families. A more compelling picture is found in a *Life* (June 1990) article titled "Children of the Damned," where we learn "there are places where childhood has ceased to exist. Where children taste crack before they taste life, then are born in a narcotic stupor. Where guns have replaced toys and a baseball bat is just another weapon." Other news stories from the Associated Press tell us how drug-addicted parents force their small children to eat garbage, revealing the sad truth that man is the only species exhibiting cruelty to its own kind.

Within the circle of my own sheltered reality, I know of one mother trying to raise four small children by herself after her husband walked out one day, never to be heard from again. I entertain a quiet rage over his behavior and harbor the uncharitable thought that he be put on the FBI's list of wanted persons and put to work breaking rocks should he be found. These four children are enrolled in our elementary schools in Shreveport. Will their teachers be able to compensate for the absence of a father's love and discipline? I don't know. All I know is that our schools may be the only real opportunity these children have for a decent life.

A friend who directs a program that places neglected and abused children in foster or adoption homes reports on a family (the term hardly applies) where the father got drunk one evening and battered his young son to death with a two-by-four. If this were not enough, the slightly older sister was witness to the horror. The father took his dead son, placed him in a bed with his bound sister, and set the house on fire to hide his evil act. The sister managed to escape and was placed in a foster home and eventually in an adopted home. Will her new family and our schools be able to erase the effects of this trauma? I don't know. All I know is that schooling may be the only opportunity for her to realize the promise in her life.

One more example. Here is a father friend of ours with three teenagers. The mother decides that she doesn't want to be married any more and just walks out one day and takes up with another man. Fortunately, these three children are through the elementary years. Will our middle and high schools help these children understand why their mother abandoned them? I don't know. All I know is that those schools may be the only opportunity for these three teenagers to develop strength out of an act of gross negligence.

Writing in *Vital Speeches* (15 June 1990), Roger Freeman offers an informing and provocative perspective on family life in our nation: "The widespread abandonment of parent responsibility for children, that began its growth in the early 1950s, is a phenomenon without parallel or precedence" (p. 515). Freeman points out that about 85% on AFDC rolls are there because parents (usually the father) fail to support them.

We can talk about national education goals, and we should. We can talk about national certification standards for teachers, and we should. We can talk about more accountability in education based on results, and we should. We can talk about shaking the bureaucracy of our schools, and we should. We can talk about lengthening the school day and the school year, and we should. We can talk about vouchers and parental choice, and we should. But if Americans believe that our schools are going to be the only salvation for the moral rot in our families, then we are a foolish and mistaken people.

Are we a "nation at risk" because of our schools? Maybe. But we are a nation at risk for many reasons other than our schools. In recent news accounts I am told that I personally — along with every other taxpayer in the nation — owe $2,000 to help the federal government bail out the U.S. savings and loan industry. The executives in this industry apparently took the S&L's into a $500 billion hole, while enjoying lavish lifestyles with million-dollar yachts, multi-million-dollar salaries, and private art collections. In this sordid display of incompetence and duplicity, these scions of free enterprise have placed an intolerable financial burden on every responsible person in our nation. Can you imagine what $500 billion would have purchased for the war on drugs, the war on poverty, and the war on ignorance and illiteracy?

My memory does not have to be especially sharp to remember other prostitutions of integrity in our national life: of defense contractors ripping off the government, of food companies deliberately diluting apple juice drunk by children for its supposed nutritional value, of pharmaceutical companies distributing defective birth-control devices, of high-pressure tactics in selling junk bonds, of national management firms participating in audit shenanigans with the very companies they are supposed to guard.

If Americans think that school-based management, or privatizing our schools, or cutting out the frills, or more early childhood programs will compensate for this moral rot, then we are a foolish and mistaken people. We beget what we value in our home life, in our economic life, and in our educational life. The values we profess are acted out in our personal and national behavior every day.

I have written these essays to celebrate the call to teaching, to honor the devoted men and women who every day give heart, mind, and soul to the children in our schools. My heart sings for the best models I have described in these essays. Let me offer one more. The daughter of an old Air Force friend of mine began teaching in a suburban school system this past year. She loves her children and her work. In her classroom is a child with an infected throat and a high fever. The family is poor and cannot afford the medical care that so many families take for granted. Focusing on high expectations, high standards, and educational results doesn't help very much in these circumstances. A loving teacher can. This teacher secured a few moments of *pro bono* medical care from a physician friend. It is for acts like these that I have penned these essays.

In *National Forum* (Spring 1966) Gregory Anrig, president of the Educational Testing Service, commenting on current reform movements in U.S. education, says:

> I learned a long time ago that you don't get people — children or adults — to improve by telling them how bad they are. Constructive change generally comes about when enough people believe it is needed and it is possible and then set about doing it together. The kind of education change needed to address the economic concerns that underlie this period of reform is instructional changes. This can only happen in the classroom and must have the support of teachers if it is to occur. (pp. 5-6)

Speaking to this point, John Goodlad, in *The Moral Dimensions of Teaching*, says:

> There is an ironic contradiction in these orgies of school reform that sweep the country from time to time. They lament the condition of our schools; frequently and in strident language, they invoke the importance of teachers, lay more demands for accountability on them — and then leave them out of the process. (p. 25)

We need the discomforting but necessary review of friendly critics in order to improve our schools. But we also need the devoted and equally necessary caring of our teachers. In a word, we must have a partnership. We need criticism of every enterprise in this nation, the schools, business, government, the health-care system, the military. But before we get ready to criticize the other fellow, let's look and make sure that all is in order in our own house before we launch our attack.

Now back to Mr. Anrig and Mr. Goodlad. Do we get folks to perform better by telling them how bad they are or by involving them in the process of improvement? Something to think about. It's essential to catch folks doing something right and reinforce them for that behavior. This is how to build a strong partnership.

A good example of what can happen in a community when folks stop criticizing and start working together was reported in *USA Today* (12 February 1987): "Boston's business, civic, and social leaders — using no federal funds — have opened thousands of jobs to inner-city youth, raised millions of dollars for scholarships and job training. Of the high school class of 1985, 93 percent are now in college or working full time." The article goes on to describe the half-dozen partnership ventures that attacked problems of jobs, dropouts, and housing. Americans are hard to beat when they turn their wills to a common task. Reminds me of that old cartoon of two mules tied together pulling in opposite directions to reach different bales of hay, when all they had to do was to turn together and eat one bale of hay at a time.

In families, in business, in schools — in every facet of our national life — we reap what we sow, realize what we value. And deciding what we value will be a matter of continuing argument and tension.

We have a promise to keep. The promise is to our children, and the promise is in our children. We do not have to demean our past to improve our future. We do not have to look back in shame nor forward in fear if we are willing to forge partnerships in which we can sustain honest criticism and reinforce the best in performance.

In *The Purposes of Education* (1976), Stephen Bailey writes, "There is more misery in this world than there ought to be, and education broadly conceived can do something about this condition." This, too, is why teachers teach.

References

Anrig, Gregory R. "Schools and Higher Education in a Period of Reform." *National Forum* (Spring 1986).

Bailey, Stephen. *The Purposes of Education*. Bloomington, Ind.: Phi Delta Kappa, 1976.

Barnes, Edward. "Children of the Damned." *Life* (June 1990).

Freeman, Roger A. "Does America Neglect Its Poor?" *Vital Speeches* (15 June 1990).

Goodlad, John; Soder, Roger; and Sirotnik, Kenneth. *The Moral Dimensions of Teaching*. San Francisco: Jossey-Bass, 1990.

"The 21st Century Family." *Newsweek* (Winter/Spring 1990).